OVER MY SHOULDER

For my loved ones
Vernon and Gwyneth
and to
the memory of my parents
Daisy and 'Ivy' (David) Jameson

Norma MacMaster

Over My Shoulder

A MEMOIR

the columba press

First published in 2008 by
the columba press
55A Spruce Avenue, Stillorgan Industrial Park,
Blackrock, Co Dublin

Cover by Bill Bolger
Origination by The Columba Press
Printed in Ireland by ColourBooks Ltd, Dublin

ISBN 978-1-85607-605-0

Acknowledgements
Special thanks to the Ardgillan Writers' Group, Balbriggan, for their
frequent 'booster-shots' and to my friend Moyra Wallace Smyth, the
world's greatest encourager.

Table of Contents

I have felt
A presence that disturbs me with the joy
Of elevated thoughts;
A sense sublime
Of something far more deeply interfused,
Whose dwelling is the light of setting suns,
And the round ocean and the living air,
And the blue sky, and in the mind of man.

William Wordsworth

CHAPTER ONE

Prelude

Cavan was my world when I was a child in the 'forties and yet not Cavan either in its frying-pan shape on the yellowing school map, but a small market-town in East Cavan where, through my child's eyes, there were just 'children' and 'people', the latter being a rough-tongued and rough-to-the-touch species in hairy tweed coats. That I loved the place is too much to say for I was not conscious of so much emotion, my feelings tending to run in tangible ways, little jets and upsurges of joy at the smallest of things. There was peace, of course, in my soul, for how else could all those far-off sights and sounds and smells and tastes have found their way into the depths of me, to knit up my being so that forever it is to be counted the heart of a Cavan child born and bred into Presbyterianism, into a large and thrifty, quietly prosperous family. There was room to grow in those days; room for roots to sink down and to send up, eventually, beautiful blooms and worthy fruits with which to nourish and sustain future generations of Cavan children, and children of other counties too.

That small town, Bailieborough, was birthplace of the grandfather of Henry and William James, of Francis Sheehy Skeffington (born in the same house, perhaps in the same room – as I and my brothers and sisters), and it fashioned *seanchaíthe* who wove their stories out of drumlin and whin, out of ragweed and thistle and the hardy people who lived off those unruly places.

There were 'seasons' then too – not as now where the year is snipped up like patchwork with snow in Summer and ice in Spring, a few days of monsoon rains followed by a few days of bitter east wind blowing over October. When I was a child, the seasons were definite, pronounced in their contours. Spring was the time of the hedgerow gradually greening with a thin film at first; the time of gazing from school windows at the tall scotch pines and knowing with sureness that we'd see the crows busily building; and all the sheughs glossy with frogspawn to be taken home in a jar with the hope that, one day, we'd see a frog emerge before our very eyes! Always, Summer brought the sultry heat that quietened the town, the heat being caught among the hills, caught as it were to dry up the sap: then men poked at the hay with their rakes and later brought it 'home' in dusty cartloads to be tramped down in lofts to make room for still more; heat made the corner-boys lazy, made them reach for their cigarettes and, with rolled-up sleeves, they lolled and smoked as, leaning against the greasy walls, they talked and talked and talked. Summer days, long and dusty, and the ditches high with cow-parsley; all sense of time lost in the half-asleep haze and then in the dewy dawns, summer dresses, courting couples, a donkey's bray. After that the Autumn, lovely and crisp and sharp with the first touch of frost; the leaves yellowing around the lakes and the harvest to be gathered home fast before the Winter gripped; a sense of urgency now in the out-lying countryside: the threshing and stooking of sheaves, the decorating of churches for Harvest Festivals followed by welcome Harvest Suppers; this urgency felt too in the town itself for 'town' and 'country' were not two entities then but one. Most of the 'small' shopkeepers owned a field or two and hence were united by this slender thread with the bigger farming community, so that the seasons, in fact, in-truded into the lives of banker and doctor, of chemist and priest, of 'children' and 'people', making them all a grand theophany: for we believed in God and in the gods in those days, singing our wordless praises in workaday harmony.

Winter united us yet further: fields and hills, invariably snow-covered by January; streets and roads a-glitter with ice; rain held off and frost gripped so hard that icicles hung every-where day and night. Pipes burst when it thawed and houses were flooded; water collected in a basin in the bathroom for a wash, froze overnight and a deep coldness filled us all; biting toes and chilblains were made only worse by holding steaming, wet feet over the smouldering turf fires. Vests in scratchy wool were worn next to the skin; fur boots and gloves by the wealthy. Knitted balaclavas and mittens were owned by almost all and the boys who had to tramp to school wearing only wooden clogs were pitied, hatless too, their heads shaved with horse-clippers to save on the barber.

Schools were bitter places: one mud-turf smouldering in the fireplace behind a big, high, black railing and the master warming his backside; sitting on our feet to keep them warm if we could, we rubbed our chilblains till they bled and huddled into our overcoats as we tried to work out sums with freezing fingers. At night, the streets shone with ice and to slide down the centre of the Main Street, feet apart, arms extravagantly splayed, was a glory indeed.

Seasons! The changes that signalled man's awareness of Time! They would roll upon us forever like waves, each coming at its appointed hour, each carrying its own splendid galaxy of sensations: seasons now gone although we still call them by their names. And, of course, when I remember childhood in that little town, it is these that are the chief instrument of my remembering for every single one of my senses carries with it tokens, real, tangible, lasting, of seasons.

When I write about that place and about my own place in it, I cannot merely record events as though transcribing them from a diary; I must set down 'atmosphere' and what is 'atmosphere' but that which is found in the accents and voices, the gleam of an eye, the shrug of a shoulder, the curl of a lip all so woven together as to form almost a vapour; for I saw and knew all kinds of people; mixed with them all; knew their voices and their gnarled hands and dirty square nails and quick kindnesses as they'd shove a penny into our own equally dirty hands and urge us to 'buy shawklet' (chocolate).

Nature, its trees, fields and mean little hills, I adored; silently and praisefully, I worshipped them without knowing that I worshipped. Is it, I wonder, commonly understood that a child can be so filled with joy, with an almost pantheistic adoration? Did anyone ever know that at times, when I was an insignificant little girl in faded skirts and darned socks, I lay sometimes on the tops of mossy banks and buried my face in the rough, bristly surfaces, desperately trying to absorb the beauty and goodness that lay around me? Certainly I never told anyone; maybe this was something everyone else did too and didn't talk about it but just in case it wasn't, I want to put it down as a historical fact that once in 1940 approximately, there lived at least one child, in that very small and most unprepossessing of counties, who silently sang and invisibly danced for sheer gladness, receiving the land as a benison, and all the fields and lakes and acres of ragweed and the little craggy whitethorns where fairies never really dwelt at all, no matter what they told us.

Oh, my little Cavan town and all little market-towns in Ireland, can you still hold fast in spite of a matted, shrunken world that lets its mucky water seep in beneath your door?

But perhaps I get carried away! For there must have been pockets of grief as well but these I truly have to dig for, only to find that they generally concerned things like being left out of a game or being teased about having to wear pin-striped pinafores cunningly manufactured by my mother out of my father's or brothers' worn-out trousers. But these were small sorrows indeed. I never knew 'death' as a child although I worried about it sometimes; nor did I know anything about adult quarrels which must, of course, have sometimes occurred, but we were protected from secrets when it was felt that these would burden us and I recall how, when the conversation at the table got interesting enough for us to listen to, my mother would make the formal announcement, 'Little pitchers have ears!' and my younger sister and I would be despatched from the room.

My mother had been a National School teacher but had to give up that profession when she married. With her customary matter-of-factness, she settled down to bear her own children: a girl, a boy, a girl, a boy after whom, perchance (or so it seemed), she decided to become a pharmacist – just like that! Or perhaps it was that more practical, fiscal reasons connected with the education of these same children drove her again to her scholar's desk! For my parents possessed a pharmacy but no pharmacist and, although a druggist himself, my father had no authority to dispense doctors' prescriptions, so with tremendous determination, courage and resourcefulness, my mother took it upon herself to fill the breach.

I can only guess at how difficult this step must have been for both my parents. Geographically it was headache enough since the nearest railway-station (the most convenient mode of travel to Dublin) was seven miles away in Kingscourt. Moreover, from an educational point of view, the project must have seemed daunting indeed: my mother, with only a primary school education followed by teacher-training in the Church of Ireland college in Kildare Place, would have known no more science than needed to teach Nature Study to little ones; and as for Latin, a major language of pharmacy in those times, she'd have had to learn it from scratch. Then, on the other hand, my father had to stay at home alone except for Saturday nights and part of Sunday when he'd be briefly rejoined by his student-wife; and single-handedly he had to oversee the running of the pharmacy, the minding of the children and family affairs in general. To help him, they employed a housemaid to run the house and a nursemaid who virtually reared those first four children who, during this time of her studies, saw my mother just one day a week. Then after four years, her goal successfully accomplished, my mother returned from Dublin for good to don her new white coat and to stand behind the counter proud of her 'M.P.S.I.' as well she should. They were a brave and noble pair, my parents.

After her return, they had two more children, myself and my younger sister Lucy, separated by two years. Now the family was complete and intact and, with five years between me and my next brother, Lucy and I were referred to as 'the babies' until we were almost twenty years old, a quaint appellation indeed!

We grew up then in that small country town and were reared with a mixture of stern Presbyterian discipline interlaced, almost calculatedly, with good humour and even impishness which somehow combined to give us a sense of both freedom and deep contentment, for contented we were. We had the run of the town with its car-free streets; we had the run of the countryside too as my father owned some small patches of land; we also had the run of our miniature farmyard behind the house and shop where lodged betimes a sow, a donkey, calves, hens, dogs, cats, ducks and sometimes turkeys and geese, with the cows moving daintily in from pasture, morning and evening, through the Main Street, to be milked and then returned to grass.

There wasn't much money in evidence for when it came to actual notes and coins, my parents were the soul of thrift itself. But it seemed as if no one had any money in those days and to make some, people had to leave the country or take the most menial of work at home. That was one reason why we, like all the other houses in the town, always managed to have a 'maid' i.e. a young girl who'd stayed at National School as long as she could and who was then 'put out to service' to earn some money for her own hard-pressed family. Since such a girl would be too young to leave for England, her first safe step to independence was to become a 'maid', and this was even seen by some as quite a lofty calling depending in turn on the social status of 'the mistress'. Maids, in fact, worked every hour that God sent and free education for all was many years away.

Having a maid left my mother free to practise her hard-won second profession and then, as perhaps they'd dreamt of, they acquired another pharmacy in Shercock, not, I believe, out of greed but out of an anxiety around the educating of all six of us to the highest level possible for, to them, education was one of the most valuable gifts they could give their children and it was my mother, I think, who was the more far-sighted of the two in this case.

It was my father, however, who used to cycle daily to the second shop seven miles away and it must have been a tough cycle in that hilly country. In winter, I remember him at around 8 am, warming his hand-knitted balaclava and gloves in front of a new little fire of sticks while the maid fried his rasher, and the icicles hung from the gutters. He often sang silly-sounding little songs that I think he invented both for our amusement as well as to keep his own spirits up. In summer, under his cloth, peaked cap, he wore a huge square of muslin which, billowing out over his face and shoulders, acted like a mosquito-net to protect him from the flies that swarmed around the lakes. We'd wave him off around 8.30 and he'd be home again in about twelve hours for his 'tea' and always with what he called a 'long bag' (sweets) for Lucy and me in his pocket. His dinner would have been sent to him in an enamel bowl in a cardboard box on the Great Southern bus and I'm sure the conductor must often have turned up his nose at the same battered old carton tied with string and smelling invariably of stew!

With my father away in the other shop, my mother oversaw 'the estate' at home, and while she could be found baking in the kitchen or at the churn in the yard, she was most usually in her white coat behind the shop-counter. As my father grew older, she herself took turns at going to the other pharmacy (indeed they must have employed another pharmacist as well) though she never cycled: she took the bus instead until the late 'fifties when we became the proud owners of a car; now she was driven in style by one of my brothers. With her usual aplomb, she did try to learn to drive but never quite succeeded to the point of being able to drive on her own and she certainly got no encouragement from either my father or her disdainful offspring! In truth, we were not a little embarrassed by her efforts: it just wasn't the done thing for a woman well over fifty to be attempting to drive cars when she should be at home doing her knitting instead of reversing machinery into the grocer's neat display of buckets on the path outside his door and causing the most horrendous clatter.

Today, writing these words, I feel almost guilty that I have no ghost to lay, no sordid secrets to disclose although perhaps there is a shadow of regret that I didn't always reflect again to others the love they shone on me.

Socially, we were just a very ordinary family, not posh, hardworking, thrifty almost to the point of self-denial; and happy in our mixed rural community where the population was mostly Roman Catholic after whom, in terms of numbers, came the Presbyterians followed by the Church of Ireland people and a handful of Methodists, and I don't recall there ever being any animosity based on religion.

CHAPTER TWO

Pre-School Memories

In the dawn of being, there is in tiny children a definite sense of kingdom and royalty, of total unassuming command. It is a time when a tiny monarch enjoys and controls a whole realm that is at peace. He invites no one in. Perhaps it is that he senses that no one would want to come in; perhaps it is that he doesn't yet know the stultifying rules about invitations and the niceties that surround them; perhaps it is that he feels that this is how the world actually is – totally devoid of rules to be obeyed and correctness to be pandered to. Whatever the reason, he keeps his world to himself. Some educators emphasise that education is all about the 'drawing out' of this small being and they make a great fuss about the Latin word *educere* and yet mostly this 'drawing out' means simply a filling with regulations and the words 'should' and 'ought'. I don't believe any child is born with a sense of the 'divine imperative'; he is free from compulsion and yet, by the time he's four years old, we tell him he must conform to a system; that he must adjust to a society often poor compared with his own internal standards.

In my own case, I am perhaps lucky to have a long memory in that I can actually catch glimpses of that innocence when I still had one foot in Eden's Garden. I can recall, however dimly, the spring of my whole life, its source and fountainhead when I had just emerged from babyhood and stood upright, a small but definite *homo sapiens*.

It seems to me that in early childhood, there are the in-between times often forgotten in the pell-mell of what is called 'real living' in later life. Small pockets of sensation and emotion, echoes from some faraway place not long departed, before birthing, before the womb itself; times that are rarely thought of, more rarely still spoken of. I have my own quiet spaces from that most spiritual of times when I lived between infancy and the rigours of

National School which challenged me and disturbed the tranquillity.

Before I went to school, I remember I was very small and very quiet. I actually remember how it was to feel both small and quiet at the age of two to three years. I can still recall how it felt to live in a very spacious, serene world, a world that had no parameters in spite of the fact that I was part of a large, noisy family.

I rummage in the attic of my head for these treasures, little cameos and faded, disjointed memories from that pre-school era. And first, I find a pram with my baby sister in it and me walking, hot – always hot – by the side, and being admonished to 'hold the pram'. It is a sticky, sunny afternoon, full of summer and I spy a bright, yellow thing on the dusty road, on the Virginia Road as it runs past the Roman Catholic Church gate. 'Yellow' is a lovely promising colour and I pick the object up; it's an empty cigarette-box although I, of course, didn't know that, and it was 'Goldflake' no doubt, for that brand had its own distinctive carton although I didn't know that then either. I look at it a little and then start to chew it. It has a new, interesting taste, very wet and thick in my mouth, and then the 'pram person' snatches it from me, my lovely golden treasure; says that it's dirty.

On yet another walk 'with the pram', the minder of me and my baby sister meets a man. I find him disappointing because he's not interested in me but only in our minder; they laugh a lot and I stand and wait; then, suddenly, as though remembering time, the minder (we call her our 'nurse') shakes me up very rudely, slaps me and I cry; so she sets me on top of the baby and runs hurriedly towards the town, to home; as we get closer, she starts to pet me but I remember knowing that she just did this because she didn't want my mother to know something. I thought she was very rough and sneaky.

Now I am actually inside the pram, sitting snugly back under the hood. Mildred, one of my big sisters, is taking me on holiday to a farm in the country. (The farm belongs to 'the Smyths' who are our friends.) Earlier in the morning she had whispered to me the secret that she didn't want to bring my little sister, she wanted only me, and I felt proud. I am quite big enough to walk but

Mildred has decided that the simplest thing to do is to pack me, our luggage (which is an oblong, yellow basket fastened with a leather strap) and her birthday-cake, all into the one vehicle (it must have been her birthday) and she warns me to hold my hands out over the cake so that the sun won't melt the icing. Then away we go, she at a run, the pram bouncing and jolting over the four-mile stretch of road, me sitting under the hood obediently minding the cake and not a word out of me. I don't remember actually arriving at the farm but we did.

Another time, I am in a cot and the cot is beside a bed; it is a little yellow wooden cot and I have a bottle of milk with a teat on it beside my head. I feel soothed and serene, asway in a hammock of sleepiness. On a different night, a little older, I am in a big, big bed and I wake up in the middle of a very dark night. I feel so very, very lonely that I cry and cry and cry; nobody comes to me and I probably fall asleep in the end, unconsoled, in the awful deluge of a world-despair that has risen up in my small being.

Now I'm running to my mother; she's sitting on the arm of an armchair and she's wearing a dark brown silk blouse with little white spots all over it. She looks lovely and warm and welcoming. I rush to her in excitement, wanting to be gathered up but, in my excitement, I wet myself, and she says, 'Tut! Tut!' and so, disappointed and annoyed with myself, I am led away by someone.

Thinking of my mother reminds me of having a 'sore leg'; 'blood-poisoning' they told me later; they also told me that at that time I was 'two-and-a-half'. I am lying on a lumpy, brown sofa in our dining-room and my mother approaches me with a white marble slab, a black spatula and some yellow ointment. I feel neither fear nor anxiety; once more just a sense that things are as they should be. My mother is the only family-member of whom I have a 'first memory': my father, my brothers and sisters seeming to have been there all the time.

Yet again I am in the long yard at the back of our house and my mother wants to take me to the garden and I want to go there with her for it's a lovely place with curly, pink roses on the walls, but ahead of me I see the sow, noisy and gargantuan with her litter and I know fear. But my mother tells me that the sow can't see me with her great ears covering her tiny eyes so I pass by trustingly.

On another age-long afternoon, I am strolling through a room quaintly called 'the nursery' (I don't know of its ever having had a baby in it!). I am singing some song I've just made up and the first line goes 'Roun' an' roun' the mounting' (I meant 'mountain'); once again I feel very small but intact and mindless; then suddenly, with a great whooshing sound, the door at the head of the backstairs into this 'nursery' opens and down on top of me floats a huge mound of dishevelled tatters, evil and terrifying. I scream wildly, frenziedly: it is the 'buggy man' (bogeyman) from the attic and now he swoops after me as I run screeching, and faint with fear, down the long, dark, windowless corridor, only to end up in the kitchen and see my brother Ernest's laughing face emerge from the tattered quilt!

This time, I'm at a Church Sale of Work. There's a nice warm fire of glowing turf in a big, black grate and there's a 'bran-dip' beside it: you pay your money and you dip for a prize. Seated contentedly beside the warm 'dip', I soon have a goodly pile of packages beside me all of which are suddenly seized upon and, unapologetically, reinserted into the tub of bran. Later on, perhaps on the same day, I am given a wax doll by someone; perhaps it came out of the 'dip'. I have no feelings of any kind about that doll and when I get home, I discover that if I break off a piece of arm and put it on the hot grate, it will sizzle and melt; so I spend a happy time melting down that doll piece by piece – it is only about eight inches long – and this time there was no one, it seems, to interrupt me!

And so it went on, days and weeks flowing together in little runnels of time, everything bathed in light and peace in those three-year-old days before I could read clocks. Perhaps it was a good thing that people thought I was too small to be taken seriously. Had they known how aware I was, how 'whole' I felt, they might have trespassed in that pool of innocence and tried to channel it at once, and without ado, into mainstream living. However, sheltered by the deception of that near-to-babyhood place, I was left alone to grow in peace, to know my first three years an untainted place, a wholesome place in which to build my life.

CHAPTER THREE

Pater Familias

Compared with today, we were so very lucky to grow up in the security of both a father and a mother who held hands together and enclosed their children in the circle made by their love.

I turn my thoughts to my father now, a parent held close to my heart but what can I say of him? He was so totally different from my mother. As a child, I remember him as a big bundle of brown maleness with a lovely smiling face and eyes. I remember the rough, gentle voice and the big hands that I was always proud to hold when we got the chance to walk together, which was not often for he was just as busy and as hard-working as my mother.

He came originally from the very east of the county, far from the new Border and carried no Orange baggage with him. The brightest in his family, he'd been singled out to leave the small home-farm to attend Rathmines School towards the end of the nineteenth century and, while a pupil there, he lived with his married sister in Ranelagh. He became a druggist, a species now extinct and was later employed by another druggist in the busy little Cavan town. Later still, he was to buy this business and accompanying house and it was to this place, he would bring his wife and raise a family.

We learned only a very tantalising little at a time, about how he met my mother at a country dance and, overall, their courtship was kept secret from us: things were more formal then and, throughout my life, I never once heard either of them address or speak of the other using Christian names; he was always referred to as 'the Boss' and she, 'the Missus'. When they were young, they were a handsome couple, not that there were even any wedding photographs (in fact, I never saw them both together in a photograph of any kind) – but she, in her teacher-training group photo, was almost beautiful; and he, in a single shot as a young man, was good-looking with a winsome, open face.

Now, my father was distinguished from other druggists in that he had an overwhelming love of animals that he treated almost as is if they were his own dumb brothers which, as we've finally begun to see, is exactly what they were. The farmers loved him and on Fair Days they came into our shop just as much to listen to his jovial stories and his extravagant, often unwittingly poetic instructions, as to buy his cures for their beasts. He loved life and he loved people and he loved a bit of fun which last, of course, lightened my mother's more serious nature.

He was a brilliant storyteller and his audience was usually his customers: better to them was he than wireless or cinema, this man with the animal-magic and the ability to spin yarns that were both hilarious and totally devoid of malice. When he laughed, his laughter left the shop and curled heartily through the whole Main Street and people stopped and smiled. 'By George!', he would roar, his strongest and favourite expletive, with the result that the cornerboys would shout after us as we ran to school: 'By George! By George!' And we'd laugh with pride.

But my father was also a worrier. He didn't ever accept that his life should end; saw death as a tyrant; didn't ever want to leave his green fields and sick animals; secretly always afraid that he'd get cancer (which he never did) and as he grew older, was wont to talk in a determinedly philosophical way about the biblically-allotted 'three score years and ten'. It depressed him to go to funerals and, being the 'man of the house', it was always his lot to represent our family, which he unfailingly did. His Sunday black hard hat would come out of its tissue paper in the box and his 'good' coat and gloves, and when the funeral was over, he'd be very quiet for awhile and then slowly talk would begin to return, but in such a way that Cavan funerals will be forever associated in my mind with long, wet, guttery lanes to inaccessible farmhouses, coffins that couldn't be got out because the doors were too small and of 'terrible wettings' that often brought about other deaths from pneumonia. But after his relatively short-lived period of gloom, he'd fall again into his natural rhythm of zest for life and he'd take out his pipe. He wasn't a 'drinking man' when I knew him but I gathered from his stories that he'd once enjoyed the 'crack' of the pub. Now, in his 50s and 60s, he had a bottle of stout and a ham sandwich every night for his supper, disdainfully refusing to switch to Ovaltine as my mother suggested. He didn't like fussy, pretentious women and always made a point of being overly polite to them. The town wags did have a story that once when a certain lady came into our shop to buy cream for dry skin, my father declaimed, handing her a jar, 'Ma'am, this would take the wrinkles out of galvanised iron!' But I doubt if this was true: he was too sensitive, too shy, to have said such a thing; and he certainly wasn't stupid. Only one woman did he address and refer to by Christian name and she was a farmer's elderly widow and, unsociable as he was in the formal sense, he actually visited her when she was dying and this at a time when it wasn't the done thing for men to visit the sick. While wondering what story may have lain behind this gesture, I was also deeply touched by it coming from him. Big, burly man that he was, he was also amazingly tender and, aside from spoiling us, his children, which he did occasionally, we saw him cycle off one icy morning with a parcel under his arm and a doll's leg sticking out of it. He'd actually gone to a shop and made this strange purchase himself and, jealously, we demanded to know who this doll was for as we had very few toys ourselves. A little sheepishly, he told us that this doll was for a child who had nothing at all and besides it was Christmas, whereupon jealousy was replaced in us by admiration of his kindness.

When it came to 'religion', (and that was always an important issue in our home), he was every bit as ardent as my mother and an equally strict Sabbatarian; he was an ordained Elder in our church and twice a year, along with the five other Elders, administered the bread and wine at Communion. How surprising it was then to learn that all of us had been baptised in our drawing-room, my father having been too shy to stand with his wife and new baby before the assembled congregation at the front of the church. There must have been an extremely agreeable minister in charge then and perhaps my father's innate charm played a part in the novel arrangement. (I recall too that the barber used to arrive with a little case full scissors to cut my father's hair in a store-room off the shop!)

Shortly after his seventy-first birthday, he began to feel un-
well and eventually we became concerned about this great
strong, laughing man who'd never been sick in his life. The doctor took to calling, taking blood-pressure, giving advice none of
which my father dreamt of taking. He visited the eye-doctor one
Fair Day when he should have been dispensing his cures: his
eyes had gone 'funny'; maybe glasses would help. He grew depressed and morose fearing real illness and he hid himself from
the medical men as long as he could, this perverse life-lover.

Then, on a Wednesday afternoon when the shop was shut for
the half-day, he took a stroke. He'd been sitting by the fire. My
mother, secretly anxious and desperate to please, was making
him pancakes, always a favourite. Suddenly he rose frantically,
gropingly, from his chair and wordlessly shuffled and fumbled
out of the room; headed for his shop, his sanctuary, as though
sure in the knowledge that, once he reached his rows of jars and
bottles, he'd be safe. But he never reached it. Just at its door, he
collapsed a great, helpless bundle. Neighbours were called in
and, somehow, they managed to carry him up the stairs to the
bed which he was never to leave again. For two weeks he lay,
tended by his wife and five children all now fully grown; only
the eldest was missing, 'waiting it out' in Canada with her own
small children. The doctor and nurse called daily. The noisy
house fell hushed and sad for we loved none better than we
loved this giant who had crashed like an oak in a forest and now
lay, partly paralysed and unable to speak. And, oh so very sadly,
we didn't speak to him for we didn't then understand that he
could hear. Once I tried to read to him from Dickens, a feeble,
frail gesture, a plea to him through a writer he had loved, to
come back to us but when he didn't respond, I closed the book.
For fourteen days and nights, he lay watching us flit about his
bed, hearing our whispers to ourselves while he faced his
mortality alone. He must have known he was dying but, in our
ignorance, we didn't reach out to share his and our own feelings
as people understand they must do today and, aside from hands
laid on his forehead and kisses on his cheeks, he didn't hear
from us.

That memory will forever pain me and yet perhaps that
would have been how he himself expected things to be – we'll

never know. When the minister called to see him and stood quietly by the bed, simply and gently saying The Lord's Prayer, my father smiled. I was twenty years old at the time and this was my first experience of death. Nowadays, so much more can be done for stroke victims but there was nothing more to be done then.

It was an April afternoon when he left. I was summoned by my mother's cry and when I entered the 'sick-room', I realised with a powerful immediacy that he simply wasn't there anymore; he was definitely somewhere but here no longer in this dim and lonesome room. So mechanically, I opened the window very wide, yellow curtains fluttering, as if to release him into the great communion of souls. A popular song drifted in from someone's wireless and the blinds all came down; the shop stayed closed and relatives were notified. His brother, Uncle Jack, was here already, had been keeping vigil for two days in spite of his eighty odd years; had been summoned by a telegram that had read, 'Sinking fast.'

How foolish it would be to try to describe grief when all of us knows it so well, but it was new to me. I was now in a very dark and very hopeless place. Helpless and hopeless. Nothing could be done to bring him back; I'd never again hear his laughter, feel the warmth of his hands. In my anguish, I looked toward 'God in his heaven' and wanted to claw the eyes out of the sky in fevered rage.

A coffin came and they placed his body in it. Black mourning clothes were produced from somewhere and my sister came from Canada – too late now. When she went into the room where the body still lay among wreaths and garlands, she surprised me with the bitterness of her protest: 'But he didn't give a damn about flowers!'

On the day of the funeral, I sensed anew the finality of his going: we wouldn't even be able to see his dead face anymore and I intimated that I must indeed follow his body to the grave or at least to the church. But in the 50s, Cavan Presbyterian women did not attend funerals, not even the funeral of a husband and father and we could only watch from an upstairs window, my mother, myself and my three sisters, as my brothers and male cousins shouldered the coffin into the waiting hearse.

Uncle Jack wept aloud. I heard no more: never knew what hymns they sang at his burial service or what words were spoken about him although I am sure the minister told us. In the evening, when the graveyard was deserted, we women went, like Christ's women, to look at the festooned grave and someone took photographs of it: I never understood why.

Next day, all seven of us, black-clothed and white-faced, assembled in the drawing-room and the family solicitor was ushered in. We sat around my mother in a half-circle. I hardly knew and didn't care what was happening but the solicitor had come to read aloud, and in the presence of us all, my father's 'last will and testament': we knew it, of course, already, for my father would have done nothing other than bestow all his worldly goods upon my mother. That little ceremony lasted about ten minutes and that, it seemed, was the end of the dying business.

Out in Urcher Graveyard, deep in the countryside, I stood alone by the newly-closed grave that still lacked a headstone and have never felt so empty in my entire life. For the first time, I knew an abyss, a void, and no holy words or thoughts came to fill it.

In those days it was the custom, following the death of a close relative, to wear 'black' for a full year and, in addition, for all the adult males to wear a black cloth diamond-shape stitched onto a jacket sleeve; they would also wear black ties. In addition, all dances, parties and cinema shows would be foregone for a year. However, we observed none of these rituals beyond the wearing of 'mourning' for a week or so – my mother for much longer – and our hearts instinctively turned away for some time from public entertainment.

In the succeeding days and weeks after the funeral, I planned secretly to follow him by the simple expedient of not eating, sure that I'd find him somewhere among the wispy clouds and the little hills where the cattle still lowed, but Life still held me firmly in its grip and forced my hand. And once, while deep in sorrow I stood in the shop idly flicking dust from a bottle, I thought I heard his voice, his laughing voice, say, 'Come on out o' that! The whole thing's not worth a ball of blue!' which were the words he'd used so often to underpin his own cheerful nature. And, of course, my sorrow wasn't worth a ' ball of blue' and death itself not worth a 'ball of blue': in other words, no matter what life cast upon us, it would all pan out in the end so we must take it on the chin! That was my da.

CHAPTER FOUR

Our Medical Hall

Unlike the modern, neon-lit emporia with their flitting white-clad figures, our Medical Hall was a dimly-lit Aladdin's Cave, dark enough and empty enough for us children to explore in secret, casual delight; only my mother, the pharmacist, wore a white coat; my father, the druggist, wore woollen jumpers with the sleeves rolled up and the 'shop-boy' wore a khaki-coloured coat.

Outside, a sign-board, with huge gilded letters, declared our home to be 'The Medical Hall' and the words, ' J. G. Gamble M.P.S.I.' meant that J.G. Gamble and *M*aggie *P*arr were *S*itting *I*nside – that little play on the initial letters indicates how novel the appended letters were in the last quarter of the nineteenth century when they were, in fact, first used. 'J. G. Gamble' was the person from whom my father bought the shop and when my mother 'qualified', the words 'D. Jameson M.P.S.I.' were added.

That small-town shop seemed always empty; a customer, a phenomenon; a 'script' something that sounded alarums; but there was time – aeons of it – for talk as well as for buying and selling.

But let me bring you inside: we cross a step worn to a 'U' shape by millions of footfalls; we swing through half-glass, black, wooden doors with polished brass handles and onto a floor made of giant stone flags. On one side is a wainscot of glass cases surmounted by a domed, glass counter upon which rests a four-foot wall of mirror, itself ornamented on top by black, curlicued, wooden scrolls. No commerce takes place on this side of the shop and the glass counter is used only to display free-standing cardboard advertisements. I remember one of these in particular: it was for Rodine Rat Poison and often, as a child, I gazed lovingly at Sir Rat who, in the picture, turned in his chair to the waiting Butler-Rat and, indicating the vacant place on his right said (majestically, I was sure), 'Dinner for one, please James. Madam will not be dining: she tasted Rodine!' Besides this, there were also the simple little ads that told us that 'Aspro' didn't harm the heart and that 'Sloane's Liniment' cured back-ache; there were ads too for 'Carters Little Liver Pills' and a great warning poster which told us that 'Spitting Spreads Tuberculosis'.

On the other side of the shop was the serving-counter (small by comparison) along with the till and the burnished wall of mahogany, glass-labelled drawers with coloured glass knobs that sometimes showed us a rainbow if they were caught by a sunbeam. Of all those glass labels, I now remember only one: 'Nux Vomica' but once I knew them all. The place was resplend-ent with giant ornate jars, high as our waists, brilliantly-coloured glass and gleaming, yellow brass! It was a hallowed place, strictly concerning itself almost entirely with healing: cos-metics were regarded with something close to contempt.

In the back was the 'Dispensing Department' which, in reality, was a much humbler area having only a bare wooden floor and hundreds of battered-looking bottles, weighing-scales of all sizes, pestles and mortars, marble slabs and spatulas, glass mea-suring-jugs and phials and a little sink. Incredibly, there was also a printing-press and several racks of printers' type for my father was also in demand for the printing of posters, dance-tickets etc.

There was so much space and so much time in those days and there wasn't a bottle we didn't sniff at or a drawer we didn't open. The jar of smelling-salts lifted our heads off; another big, deep drawer was full of giant poppy-heads and then there was Epsom Salts and Glauber Salts all of which had to be sifted (a job done in the yard), then weighed and packaged and labelled; there were mustard plasters (broad as your back), carrageen moss; slushy, green soft-soap; the 'Leeches Jar' (now empty) and the 'Poison Press' always tightly locked and terrifying even at that. There were mysteries too: gadgets made of glass and rub-ber and 'trusses' for which men came to be fitted (in private) by my father; and, in a store, the barrels! These were gargantuan things containing stuff like linseed oil and paraffin and there was that awful day when my brother John turned on the tap of the treacle-barrel and forgot to turn it off!

It was a truly wonderful place that shop, with its diverse and enchanting smells and its liquids bright and alluring. And yet the highlight of all was the getting of a 'script'! When this came, the piece of paper was first carefully scrutinised by my mother for it invariably contained a long list of ingredients which the doctor deemed would effect a cure; all instructions for both dispensing and using the medicine were in a kind of shorthand Latin and I recall being very pleased to discover, using my school Latin, that t.i.d. meant 'three times a day' and that p.c. meant 'after food'! The contents of the 'script' examined, out would come the pestle and mortar and the tiny glass scales that lived in its own glass cabinet complete with miniscule weights and tiny glass pans; measuring-phials would appear and liquids of various hues would be measured; infinitesimally small amounts of powder tap-tapped from a spatula onto a weighing-pan, not a grain too many or too few. If it was an ointment that was to be made up, the marble slab came out and the measured ingredients placed on it carefully, all to be finally bound together with a spatula and then boxed in little round, cardboard boxes with close-fitting lids made for that purpose.

Watching my mother 'fill' a prescription was better even than watching her making the Christmas cake! And after the bottling or boxing of the 'script's' ingredients, came the wrapping up; the snowiest of white paper was used and with deft fingers, she would make the creases as sharp as razor-blades; lastly, with the stick of red wax, she'd put a blob of seal on the final fold, her triumphant signature. There was a machine for making pills too but I saw this in use only once when my brother, Ernest, was a pharmacy-apprentice and had to roll out and make pills as part of his training. On average, there might have been maybe six prescriptions a day.

Other customers came for lesser things. One old wag came in the evening (we closed at 9 pm and at 11 pm on Saturdays) to ask for tuppence worth of the laxative Beecham's Pills and appended that she was 'goin' dancin''! Another came to hand in a set of false teeth she'd found on the footpath; another to report a bee-sting. On one occasion, a 'lady's parcel' was demurely requested – this long before tampons or self-service. Occasionally, an 'order' would come in and then my mother would take over,

preparing a huge parcel of cotton-wool rolls and lint and sani-
tary-towels, all the while deep in confidential woman-talk with
the customer (it was always a woman in these cases) and no, we
children didn't know anything about 'Birthing' then.

There was room for originality too: bad coughs and gastric
ailments were cured by my father's home-made cough-elixir
and his 'stomach-bottle' both of which were famous throughout
a couple of counties; a recurring headache would disappear
almost as soon as he pronounced the majestic words: 'Acid
Acetylsalicylic' which sounded much better than plain 'aspirin';
while 'sore feet' were once creatively attended to by an inspired
shop-girl who mixed boric powder with charcoal, packaged it
and labelled it 'Grey Foot-powder'! She seemed pleased with
her ingenuity but I don't know if there was ever a repeat sale of
the product! Nonetheless, most of the cures worked: such was
the faith of our customers in the lavish, sympathetic understanding found in The Medical Hall.

When it came to animals, my father ruled alone and
supreme: he had old 'receipts' for such afflictions as the scour,
blackleg, red-water, hoose, foot-rot, the botts etc. and he dis-
pensed these cures majestically, scooping up his crystals, pour-
ing out the liquids and funnelling the lot into waiting five-nag-
gin bottles or folding them into neat parcels, all the while regal-
ing his farmer-customers with stories and then, finally, before he
handed over the medicine, would come the words we secret lis-
teners always waited for: 'Put a lump of fat bacon under her
tongue and bottle it into her!' And that was the climax of his mir-
acle-working! And it did all seem miraculous. On a Fair Day, the
shop would be packed with farmers looking for their miracles
and all day long, he would mix and measure, doling out bottles
and advice. Sometimes a calf or a bullock would barge in between the glass counters and, with ash-plants and much noise,
it'd be driven out again. At other times, even in the small hours
of the morning, anxious farmers would knock him up to attend
to a sick beast and he would pedal six, seven or more miles in
the dark with the medicine in his pocket. He was such a person-
ality that tributes and stories about him have been recorded by a
seanchaí and stored in the National Archive.

Life moved slowly then and, as we grew older, we dosed

ourselves with this and that and never went near a doctor. When penicillin arrived, we'd suck a lozenge as we passed the jar on the shelf just in case we might be getting a sore throat! And John, who was studying to be a vet, took down the water-filled phosphorous jar one day and, in the absence of overseers, took out a stick of it and drew it with his foot across the wooden floor of the Dispensing Department: I recall watching in awe the trail of fire that followed it!

But I suppose it was the day the fridge arrived that the century heaved and turned over and bore, to some degree, The Medical Hall with it! The fridge was first installed in the kitchen, not for food mind you, but to hold the new and totally wondrous 'sulpha' drugs. After that, change seemed inexorable: the phone came next and then Ernest 'qualified' and the old dark place of wooden floor and mystery gave way to neon lights; bottles were now sealed – no more ecstatic feasts of smells – and 'scripts' were 'filled' from mass-produced bottles and boxes delivered ever more frequently by pharmaceutical companies. The mahogany drawers went to ornament a wall in the interior of the house and the old flagged floor was replaced by something bright and blue; an artefact called a 'gondola' stood centre-front, and when my brother's son in turn 'qualified', the inevitable computer appeared.

These days when I visit, I miss the feeling of sanctuary that offered both verbal and medicinal balm and yet am impressed by the stacks of 'scripts' that stand neatly packaged in little bags with computer-printed labels all waiting collection. Yes! The pharmacists are still there but the gentle wizards are gone.

CHAPTER FIVE

Learning Irish and other Things

I didn't learn much Irish in the Junior Room of our National School (the Model School). It was full of the noise and chanting from English Readers. We chanted such lofty sentences as 'Ned put his leg in the tub' and 'The cat sat on the mat'. The final couplet of just one poem stays in my mind: it goes:

But we who are Irish
Should always be
Tidy when we sit down to tea.

which was the work, possibly, of some civic-minded educator in the Department trying to clean up our racial image.

That little sun-bright room with the orange blind was always full of the quiet jostling of small bodies as they counted out cowry shells, rolled out plasticine and recited tables in a musical, if rather doleful, rhythm. We sang songs too but in English, mournful songs like 'My Grandfather's Clock' and 'Oft in the Stilly Night', songs that brought tears to my eyes, songs that hadn't been written to cheer young hearts. I don't recall singing Irish songs in that room but I do remember trying to memorise the spelling of words from thumbed and greasy Irish Readers, words strange and difficult in themselves but made a hundred times worse by the sudden appearance of a tiny dot over a letter: when this dot appeared, we had to pause in the middle of our spelling to name it 'Shave-a-hoo!' (which was exactly how I always saw it in my head but that wasn't, of course, how it was spelt!) before proceeding with the next letters of the word.

When I graduated to the Senior Room at the age of eight, education took a sudden and much more serious turn. Now we became the owners of hard-backed, dun-coloured 'readers' in both Irish and English, books dull and uninspired. The English one to which I looked hopefully was full of pieces about Patrick Pearse and The Great Famine, about how the steam-engine was invented and about a journey to the new airport in Dublin from the centre of the city: this particular piece began, 'Fares please! We are in the long green bus that takes us from O'Connell Street to Collinstown Airport.' It might as well have been talking about a take-off to the moon, so removed was it from us country children most of whom had never even seen Dublin and were quite unlikely ever to visit the 'airport'. There was also the occasional bit of poetry in that book: William Allingham's 'Airy Mountain' was bound to be included along with Goldsmith's 'Village Schoolmaster'. The Irish Reader was much worse than the English one: full of lengthy tales, in the strange and angry-looking lettering of the 'old Irish' alphabet, about still more heroes (what little Nationalists they were determined to make us!), about the 'Salmon of Knowledge', 'A Fair Day', 'The Shoemaker', 'St Patrick', and 'Turf-cutting'. As for Irish poetry, it was always faithfully represented by 'Mise Rafterí', the blind poet.

We were also introduced to 'Carty', who had written seemingly endless history-texts, all little soft-backed books with the occasional black-and-white head-and-shoulder 'photograph': Cromwell, I remember in particular and thought he didn't look all that bad aside from his crooked nose and stringy hair. Geography texts were in blue hard-backed books and were written by Miss E. Butler; these were equally dull and uninspiring although I'm sure it wasn't the fault of either Mr Carty or Miss Butler that their books (no doubt excellent) were published in such boring editions. In the Senior Room, we were also introduced to the 'tonic solfa' in singing lessons, to 'compound interest' and to what has forever remained a wonderland to me, 'stocks and shares'!

Only a very little religion was taught as we all attended Sunday School on a regular weekly basis all the year round (if Christmas Eve fell on a Sunday, we attended Sunday School even on that day; likewise with St Stephen's Day) but apparently it was still decreed nonetheless that 'religion' be taught in our National School also. 'Religion' as a subject probably came around once a week and before the teaching of it a certain little ritual had to be performed: on the classroom wainscoting, suspended from a nail, hung a stout card (roughly sixteen inches by six). This card had the words 'Secular Instruction' printed on one side in bold blue letters; the other side read, 'Religious Instruction' and without fail, without command or question, a pupil always rose to turn the appropriate side outwards. Only many years later did I learn that this was done to protect any 're-ligious minority' that might have, somehow, infiltrated us; just in case any Jews or Muslims or Roman Catholics or even Buddhists might have got in among us in the county of Cavan and be contaminated by our doctrine! If there had, these were to be regarded as legitimately excused from the religion-lesson in the classroom just so long as that stout notice on the wainscoting said 'Religious Instruction'. No one, of course ever actually left the room simply because we were all Protestants together – the Roman Catholics had their own schools and I doubt if anyone in our town or county had ever seen, let alone known, Jew or Muslim! Still this was the law of the land then, and such a card would have been hung in all National Schools throughout the State.

So our textbooks were devoid of colour and our only 'visual aids' were two faded, political wall-maps, one of Europe and one of Ireland and we stood in semi-circles round these maps and learned that trains stopped at Mallow Junction and that there was a place faraway called 'Constantinople'. There was also a globe and with the help of this and his own ingenuity, the 'master' showed us that the earth did indeed go round the sun. And yet, on the other hand, and behind glass, in tall locked cup-boards, lay things that seemed to tell us that, once upon a time, 'school' had been a more interesting place: there was a collection of birds' eggs in nests, long-necked, glass flasks and whole sets of gilt-edged books all replaced, perhaps, in the education of young minds, by the new and urgent interest in the Irish lang-uage; in any case, these cupboards were never opened except for two things – to take out the sinuous, yellow cane when someone was deemed to be in need of it or to extract the set of little black Bibles used in 'religion'.

We girls returned to the Junior Room every Monday after-noon to learn to sew, something I truly hated, and all the boys went into the Senior Room where they were supposed to do something creative but usually did sums. In sewing-class, we had to prepare a 'book of specimens', samples of all the stitching we had mastered and which, I presume, were looked at by an inspector at some stage. 'Specimens' were my special nightmare. To prepare one, we were given a neatly-cut little piece of bright, blue calico and a length of equally bright, red thread, a mean device, I thought, to show up ugly stitches. Then after that and throughout the year, we were required to produce samples of 'run-and-fell' seams, 'back-stitch' and 'blanket-stitch'; to 'hem and tack' as well as be able to show how to mend 'hedge-tears' and how to patch things. I was quite useless with a needle and my little cloth squares always ended up soiled with the sweat of grubby hands and dotted with the blood where I'd pricked my fingers. Knitting was as bad because no matter how hard I tried to keep the stitches running freely, they'd gather in a tight, damp knot on the needles and some would get 'lost' and fail to be accounted for, thereby winning me the teacher's fury. To this day, I believe she thought I was simply being perverse when it came to needlework and that I was just too stubborn to try harder even with the help of a few good thumps on the shoulder!

Of all the subjects taught, I found Irish the trickiest and, although I didn't hate it as I did 'sewing', it still blighted my life. 'Irish': this dark thicket of largely unpronounceable words! It wasn't too bad when we simply had to read aloud from our Readers but when it came to conjugating verbs and declining nouns, my classmates and I were hopelessly lost. 'An cat. An cat. Earball an chait. – The cat. The cat. The tail of the cat', we'd chant gloomily and then fail to produce the rest of the noun's cases or the grisly moods and tenses of the verbs. 'Chuaidh mé – I went' was one thing and so indeed was 'an cat' but 'aimsir gnáth-láithreach (present continuous) and 'an modh coinialach' (conditional mood) was quite another! And oh! how we had to struggle not to get slapped for our inability to pronounce these horrendous, meaningless phrases that hadn't the remotest thing to do with our lives of 'Dandy' and 'Beano' and hopscotch and liquorice-pipes.

Basically, the 'master' was a very kind and gentle person but teaching Irish to the required standard always seemed to put him under fierce pressure, so that by the end of the lesson his face and neck would be flushed. Of course, he'd have been aware that the quality of his teaching would be tested by an inspector who'd, once a year, ask us to display our knowledge. Indeed sometimes the pressure would be so great that if the master heard on the grapevine the day the inspector was due, he'd ask the weaker pupils to take that day off which, needless to say, would be a great pleasure to them! And oh! wasn't life so easy, so laid-back, and so generous with its time in those days that no one ever minded, either parents or pupils, and the inspector would go away as innocently as he'd come, his duty done.

It was a happy school to learn in but there were few encouragements to be creative, some of which consisted, in the Junior Room, in our rolling out long, long snakes of plasticine and of turning plasticine balls into little people. Once we were shown how to make dolls by stuffing cloth shapes with sawdust and, one summer, we were allowed make little round flower-beds to grow nasturtiums and London Pride. And yet we did create as, I believe, children will always create if they are loved and cared for. We, for example, invented the most brilliant games, we even wrote our own plays and acted them out, and we wined and dined in exotic hotels drawn in chalk on the concrete where water was turned, not into wine, but into dazzling drinks using coloured crepe paper.

Such was the backdrop to our primary education but, in the Senior classroom, there was one Irish lesson, however, that will be etched forever on my mind and that's probably because it was accompanied by a very simple 'visual-aid'! It happened one day, at noon to be precise, when the master was about to open the lunch-basket that always arrived on his desk at mid-day, sent down from his digs in the town. There the basket sat, as usual, an aroma of stew emanating from the bowl that was tucked under a check tea-cloth. That day for once, I remember, the master hesitated before removing the cloth, paused as if he'd just had a brainwave. We continued to sit demurely in our desks, drawing neat boxes round the sums we'd just finished while keeping an eye on proceedings at the same time for we sensed that something new was in the air. Next thing, he hurriedly whispered something into a boy's ear and that boy (I forget who it was) shot out the door and up the street returning about five minutes later with a brown paper bag. The master was all smiling, grateful effusion, ' Go raibh maith agat – ah, thank you,' he almost simpered and we went on sitting in our seats, unmoved, waiting to be dismissed for our own lunch and yet hoping not to be despatched before this piece of drama had unfolded fully, for 'drama' it was promising to be! The master looked almost lovingly at that brown bag, feeling it, and then slowly to our growing interest, he drew out a long-necked black bottle with a yellowish, oval label that bore the picture of a harp and a black squiggly signature. Stout! We recognised it at once, had indeed already been warned against it. He held it up in one hand, a corkscrew in the other.

'Cad tá orm?' he asked us in Irish, 'What's wrong with me?' He beamed down at us.

Silence. We hadn't a clue what was wrong with him: he seemed grand. And he still beamed, for once not insisting on an answer from the total hush and then, wrestling a little with the cork, he eased it gently out: it hardly popped. He held the bottle up with affection and you could barely have heard us breathing. It was an inky-black bottle and again he called down to us in ringing tones, 'Cad tá orm?' Again a silence that was now solemn and wide-eyed. Finally, and in his most magisterial voice, he declared, ' Tá tart orm – I am thirsty!' And he put the bottle to his lips. We sighed almost gratefully as if slaking our own thirst while he took a long, long gulping swig. Then he wiped his mouth with the back of his hand and in his normal voice, as if nothing at all had happened, he called out, 'Seasaigí! – Stand! – Iompaigí! –Turn!' And thus marshalled, we ran out breathlessly for our own lunches.

That teacher and all my National School teachers are gone and grace our schools no more. With all their idiosyncrasies and frequent, careless disregard for rules, they were usually gentle, clever people with a genuine love of learning for its own sake and were often, no doubt, frustrated by the lard of bureaucracy that had begun to clog the wheels of education in this relatively new, and sometimes defensive Free State. Those teachers played an extremely important part in our lives and, without all the modern aids to learning, they frequently had to be proficient actors and entertainers as well as everything else. They taught us the facts as they knew them but added their own gloss; they disciplined us with a cane if they saw fit but they also, somehow, taught us how to sit easy to life, how not to be overwhelmed by it. Sometimes they made us cry but they always flipped the coin and brought back laughter. Neither we nor our parents doubted but that they were good people who were called upon not only to fill their roles as teachers but who were often required to play an active part in church life as well, whether they liked it or not.

On the day we got our summer holidays, that teacher who had once sent for stout, invariably sent for a large consignment of sweets, paid for, no doubt, out of his own never-too-full pocket and these he'd scatter among us with something like gaiety: holidays were, for him as well as for us, 'the pearl of great price', and in that final hour we'd give him three cheers, all united together in what we felt was a freedom hard won. In that hour, I think we loved all teachers.

CHAPTER SIX

She

A versatile lady, not beautiful or handsome except in a chiselled fashion. Versatile and many-sided. A prism to catch light, to break up its colours. She could knit socks for soldiers with grey, greasy war-time wool or pick out robins' eggs in hedgerows, chase rats with a sweeping-brush, decipher a doctor's prescription and, grain by grain, drop by drop, make up a medicine. She could teach equations, knew how many yards were in a mile, how much butter in a firkin, make butter too, swishing it round in its barrel before slapping it into oblongs stamped with her seal of flowers. She sewed coats and bonnets fit to be seen in church, and turned her man's trousers into pin-stripe pinafores for wearing to school. Her tongue was as sharp as a razor, or soft and gentle when speaking of women who'd suffered and of little children. Laces and gorgeous embroidery flowed from her fingers that, at other times, counted the hard-won notes in the till. Knew the Bible by heart; tried to live by its rule; could leave a cleric standing on the footpath having banged the door in his face at some fancied insult to her God. Not vain but dyed her hair from bottles kept in the same cupboard as her 'Mission to Lepers' boxes. Took life in her stride: sickness and health; new babies and dead lambs; decaying flesh and bursting hedgerows; all welcome; all received with grave acceptance; these were the things she'd been born for. Loved a laugh though few knew it, her laughter a secret left over from her girlish past when she'd scarce turned twenty. She played the piano a little and the harmonium too. Sang songs but the voice had long since cracked and broken. Had two careers, was teacher and chemist, had six children, a devoted husband and a good brain. Fearless. No fear of a single thing in her entire being. Majestic, therefore. A thing to be leaned on. Stalwart and ever-present whether to succour, cajole or chastise. A thing. A rock. Under her shadows, life was lived in abundance; not frugally but with careless abandon. She'd always be there, great wings outstretched. Then, one day, she wasn't there. She. She had gone. Had had the temerity to leave off. She'd been my mother.

CHAPTER SEVEN

Growing up a Presbyterian on the Border in the 40s

We are different. I've always known that. My family tells me so; and my church echoes both tellings.

But they are happy days. I attend a two-room National School where only Protestant children go and there aren't many of us: boys and girls together. The Roman Catholics have two schools: one for boys and one for girls. We have just one Roman Catholic playmate and she has some strange ways which we neither question nor deride. For example, she talks about something called 'devotions' and 'the rosary'; she talks about 'mass'; we don't understand these things. In her house, little red lights burn eerily in front of ugly pictures of hearts that drop blood but we are reluctant to quiz her about these things either. We just assume that they are part of the trappings of this foreign, distant but, somehow, very powerful R.C. church to which we are relieved we don't belong. (I write these things down as I see them with my child's eyes.) I have never been inside her chapel (but I could have if I wanted to) and her religion does not allow her enter my church. Roman Catholic missioners come to the town sometimes and they curiously have nights for men only and other nights for women only and it is then that we hear talk about them 'running to the chapel' as against ourselves just 'going to church'.

Our playmate goes to what she calls 'confessions' as well and we wonder what she could have to confess and what it might be like to talk to a priest in a box. Our mother tells us that Roman Catholics have to confess their sins to a priest but that we must confess only to God. Our religion seems to have very few rules, hers a great many. There are 'fast days' and 'holy days of observation'; there is 'Lent' and all kinds of Saints' Days; there are 'mortal sins' and other kinds of sins that I don't know the names of.

We Presbyterians have no holy days at all except Sunday which we very often refer to as 'the Sabbath'; also Easter Day which, of course, is always on a Sunday; and maybe we'd count St Patrick's Day but we don't hold with 'saints' at all really; even 'Paul' in the Bible is just plain 'Paul'. And we don't observe Lent although we are always very curious to see Roman Catholics going about on Ash Wednesday with black smudges on their foreheads. Is it done with burnt paper, we wonder? The 'Church of Irelands' (my mother used to be Church of Ireland) have Saints' Days and Lent but not us Presbyterians, and no Protestants, of any variety, believe in Purgatory or Limbo. Protestants in our town consist mostly of us Scots Presbyterians but there are a fair few Church of Irelands and a handful of Methodists. (Only my mother is allowed take Holy Communion in the Church of Ireland Church even though she has been Presbyterian from the time she married my Presbyterian father. The rest of us can't go with her, for example, to Communion on Christmas Day, so she always has to go alone.)

But back to the Catholics – we don't know what people mean when, after a funeral, they say that the 'offerings' was x number of pounds, but I think it has something to do with purgatory which sounds a frightful place and, in my child's mind, it seems that important people stand a better chance with God when they die. And what can it possibly mean to be 'read off the altar'? We ourselves have no altars at all, only a Communion Table. Also we don't make the 'sign of the cross' (we wouldn't know how!) and we don't heed the Angelus. Roman Catholics stop and pray in the street when the bell rings at noon and men take off their caps. I think that this is a nice custom. Roman Catholics go to dances on Sundays and, after Mass (which they *have* to attend), they can go to football matches and read the Sunday papers. They have a lot more fun on the Sabbath than we do although we know they shouldn't. We can't do anything at all on a Sunday except go to church (twice! and also once to Sunday School – three hours in all). But it isn't a sin for us not to go to church; we can go for walks or make family visits but we can't play in the street and we can't play board-games like draughts; knitting or sewing even for fun is forbidden although letters can be written just so long as they are to family or friends and nothing to do with business. My father sometimes cheats, however, and listens to an 'All-Ireland' on the wireless.

In school, our Readers sometimes have poems about 'Mary' or 'the Queen of Heaven'; our teacher skips these and we understand that she is right to do so. Outside, in our playground, we sometimes hear the master of the boys' Roman Catholic school teaching 'Catechism' and we stand, wickedly listening: he shouts and strikes, and big boys whom we've seen swaggering on the streets bawl and cry. I feel sort of sad myself then, sad for the boys. Once I heard that Roman Catholics are taught that we don't believe in the 'Virgin Birth' but we do.

Unlike the R.C.s and the Church of Irelands, we have no priests or bishops. We have a Minister who along with the Elders governs our congregation which itself has voted in the Elders who are then ordained. The Head of our Church is called a Moderator and there's a new one appointed each year and also elected by the people. The Moderator sometimes wears things like gaiters and a frilly shirt. Roman Catholics have priests and canons and their Pope.

We have never, ever seen the Canon in our town but we gather he is a fearsome personage. Most of all, however, we are fascinated by nuns. In the summer, we see them walking the roads in their black garb, with stiff white head-and-chest pieces. We hear they have no hair, that it has been all shaved off; we hear that before they took their 'final vows', they had to spend a whole night lying in an open coffin in the church; we hear they never live with their families again. We listen to them at play in the Convent Garden and can't imagine how grown women can giggle and throw a ball around like children. Sometimes they stop in their walks to talk to us but we feel smug knowing what they are up to and knowing we are safe from them. (We feel that the whole mishmash of priests and bishops, canons and nuns are out to lure us into their clutches.) We are not terribly interested in ordinary priests except for just one who is (oh! so strangely!) a friend of my parents. There are just some contradictions that we children do not question. We all seem to get along well together but I sense that there is a wall between us, underneath, but that we mustn't even mention a wall; we must simply pretend that it isn't there.

In Sunday School, we learn Bible stories (we hear Roman Catholics aren't allowed the Bible and we pray for them) and we learn whole psalms off by heart. We are not taught that Roman Catholics are bad people, only that they are deluded and I think the Pope and the priests are in a kind of conspiracy against them.

Our church is very plain inside; there are no ornaments or pictures or crosses or candles although we do have one lovely stained-glass window showing Jesus as the Good Shepherd, right beside our family pew. Once someone wanted to paint the arch behind the Communion Table a pale blue and this caused some friction in the congregation because 'blue' was considered to have some connection with Mary; we like and respect Mary but we never worship her. We have Communion only twice a year: on the first Sundays in May and November; if we had it more often, it might, perhaps, lose some of its solemn meaning and be taken for granted. We children don't go to Communion yet, not until we are at least twelve years old. We hear that Roman Catholics believe that the bread and the wine are really turned into flesh and blood. I think this is disgusting and I am glad again that I am not an R.C. We are also very strict about not swearing by God's name.

Roman Catholics don't attend our social gatherings and we don't attend theirs. Aside from my one Roman Catholic play-mate's, I have never been inside a Roman Catholic house. A Presbyterian girl starts to go out with a Roman Catholic man and a terrible cloud descends on our congregation. We hear she is 'receiving instruction' which means that 'they' are making her give up her own religion which she has to do if she wants to marry him; and all her children will have to be Roman Catholics too. Why couldn't *she* make him turn to be a Presbyterian in-stead? There is a lot of talk about 'turning' and then this talk just fades into angry silence.

On Remembrance Day, we wear poppies in our coats in re-spect for our ancestors who died to give us freedom and some-times these poppies are snatched from our lapels and stamped on the ground. We sometimes quarrel, but not often, with the Roman Catholic children and then generally for no good reason: it is just 'us' and 'them'. They shout, 'On St Patrick's Day, we'll be merry and gay and we'll kick the oul' Protestants outa the way!' and we retaliate, 'Up the long ladder; down the short rope; up with King Billy; to hell with the Pope.' We also have a riddle that goes, 'Which would you rather have – the prod of a needle or the lick of a cat?' and when we say 'the lick', we jeer each other about rather being a 'cat o' lick'!

We don't know much about either the Pope or King Billy except that the Pope, the Head of the Roman Catholic church claims *never* to be wrong and that King Billy defeated King James at the Boyne where it flows near Drogheda shouting, 'Come on, ya Bap ya!' at the disgraced king. We make no more than a passing connection between King Billy and the Orange Parades, or 'walks' as we call them, which are held in various farmers' fields on the Twelfth; a good few buses with pipe-bands go to walks in the North but there is no great fuss about these activities. I touched an Orange sash once – it was made of very stiff, silky stuff and had little silvery ladders on it; there was stuff on it out of the Bible too. In our attic is a picture of King Billy mounted on his white horse and busily plunging about in the Boyne waters; his blue coat has real, dazzly stuff on it that falls off when we pick at it. The picture doesn't really belong to our family; it just, somehow, happens to be there and I don't know where it came from. Our parents aren't very interested in Orange sashes or walks but my mother, in a frivolous mood, will sometimes sing (wistfully, I think) a quaint song about 'Dolly's Brae' – but she doesn't even know all the words anymore.

And so we grow. We hear our elders talk about the 'Free State' but we don't really know what that means and when our mother sends us to the shop for thread, she warns us to ask for 'English' thread, not 'Irish'. We know that sweets from Northern Ireland must be better; must for some foreordained reason *be* better; the schools up there are better: a cousin in Armagh is learning French and she is only nine. We have an aunt in Belfast who jeers our mother for living 'down here' and our mother gets very cross because we know she'd much rather be living in Belfast and she grows almost white with rage when this same aunt sneeringly sings a silly song about 'hanging out your washing on the Free Sate line'. My father is much less prickly about these affairs but it is only years later that we are to know my mother's story: to know that once upon a time, when she was a girl, a young woman, a river called the Woodford River flowed right past the very end of her garden, my grandparents' garden, and it had a bridge over it at Aghalane (a bridge one day to be blown up by the IRA) and without as much as a 'by your leave', an invisible border was drawn at the bottom of that garden, cutting her off from the neighbours who lived on the other side of the river, they now to live in one country and she in another. Instead of walking a hundred yards to visit them, she now had to go miles although they continued to go to the same church. Her nearest big town, the fairyland of her childhood, Enniskillen, was stolen from her forever. She carried these hurts to her death.

So we know our Roman Catholic neighbours and yet we don't know them at all. Some of them tell us we aren't even Irish and yet we know we are – what else can we be? We love our country and hate Cromwell and the English who have done so many bad things to us; we like to learn the Irish language even though it is hard; we sing our National Anthem with pride and we wear our sprigs of shamrock on St Patrick's Day. But we feel at odds somehow; we are, as they say in Cavan, standing with one foot in Mullagh, the other in Moynalty; not belonging here, not belonging there; and we don't feel very much anymore either, except a little uneasy; always uneasy. Perhaps the very insecurity of this uneasiness makes us strong but we don't know; we don't really know much about anything (is that called 'losing your identity?') – maybe that's why we don't speak out enough. We are really a Janus, that two-headed dog, all the time looking North to our brothers and sisters on the other side of the Woodford River, stock of our stock, but also to the South, to our friends and neighbours. A lost and schizoid people. But that sounds sad and, strangely, 'sad' is something we most definitely are not, whatever else we might be.

CHAPTER EIGHT

Learning to be Religious

Whether it was part of a strategy to hang on at all costs to our Presbyterianism, rooted in Calvinism and constantly under siege by the Roman Church, or whether it was solely a genuine human response to the entire pulsating cosmos, doesn't really matter but what it meant, in practical terms, was that religion in its boxed and rigid form was introduced into our lives at a very early age. I can't remember a time when the words 'God' and 'Jesus', 'Bible' and 'Communion' were pronounced with other than awe. At the age of about three, I recall chanting The Lord's Prayer as though it were a nursery-rhyme: 'Our Father which shart in heaven ...' a 'shart' being what I then also called the long orange-painted handle of a farm-cart.

As children, we spent one hour every Sunday in Sunday School followed by two more in church, one in the morning and one in the evening. We spent another hour on Saturdays and about thirty minutes a week in National School all in being indoctrinated. 'Indoctrination' is a word that has only fairly recently earned itself a bad reputation, especially when it came to be associated with cults, but the 'indoctrination' of the 30s and 40s was, I think, simply a sincere, harmless and methodical way of ensuring that what were seen as eternal values and ways of looking at God were passed on safely and in full measure to the next generation. Moreover there was a definite pride attached to being 'Presbyterian': we were proud of our faithfulness to our tradition in spite of 'famine and sword', proud that we had withstood the onslaughts of the once-established Anglican Church and the Roman Church, proud of our values – our thrift, our industry, our stern sense of duty, our honesty.

These were ideals, of course, and whether we always lived up to them was another matter. There was nothing sinister, therefore, about our indoctrination; in fact, in those days in

Cavan, it was much more suspect to be taught nothing at all about God, the great Jehovah, a God mostly stern and heavy-browed although laughing betimes; and it was at that time infinitely healthier to be taught about him from any denominational point of view than not at all. In fact, come to think of it, I never met one single person who hadn't been given a rigorous religious education of one kind or another until I went to University and then it was the son of a professor who found my still fervid belief in God (as he'd been taught me) not a little quaint!

Our Sunday School was conducted in the 'Meeting House' (as Presbyterians often called their place of worship) and it was held immediately before the main morning service. In those days, there would have been about thirty children, all clean and shiny, shoes gleaming, and we were separated into three classes, each to occupy a corner of the church building, to sit demurely in its oak pews. 'Sunday mornings' always had their own special feel: they were 'best china', 'best linen' taken from the musty drawer of the week; they were shining and precious and awesome, a bit unreal and a bit too other-worldly.

There were two catechisms: there was 'The Child's Catechism' which questioned the youngest of us on ancient biblical myths and stories so that we'd remember them for all time:

'Who was the first man?'

'Adam.'

'Who was the first woman?'

'Eve.'

'Of what did God make Adam?'

'Of the dust of the ground.' And so the questions went on through Moses, Methuselah, Elijah and so on.

There was also 'The Shorter Catechism' which was presented to us at the age of eight (so very many things seemed to toughen up at that tender age); this one made me wonder what the 'longer' version must have been like, this shorter one being so hideously difficult. A neat little soft-backed book with a fawn cover, it was handed down to us, comfortably thumbed and greasy like the rest of our books. The most interesting thing about it, I thought, was the ad on the back cover which read, 'They come as a boon and a blessing to men, the Pickwick, the Owl and the Waverley pen.' This ad and the very first question is absolutely all that I can remember of the text of this catechism in spite of the many hours spent learning its contents by rote:

Q: What is man's chief end?

A: Man's chief end is to glorify God and enjoy him forever.

I still have that little book, an antique now, and I sometimes refer to it just to muse over the tortuous wording (that often rolled delightfully in one's mouth even though not understood) and the difficult theological concepts which we, as young children, were expected to grasp. I look at it just now beside me, the worn yellow pages seeming sad and deflated as if it knew that its wisdom had never really hit the mark in the first place and the name 'Mildred Jameson' claiming ownership.

The cover, with its now almost illegible print, says that it has been written by one Rev Roderick Lawson and printed in Edinburgh; astonishingly, the 'Preface' says that it is 'intended for those of weaker capacity'! What nit-wits we must have been! And it has one hundred and seven questions, a couple of which run like this:

'What is repentance unto Life?'

Answer: 'Repentance unto Life is a saving grace whereby a sinner out of a true sense of his sin and apprehension of the mercy of God in Christ, doth with grief and hatred of his sin, turn from it unto God with full purpose of, and endeavour after, new obedience.'

And another: 'Wherein consists the sinfulness of that estate whereinto man fell?' with the answer, 'The sinfulness of that estate whereinto man fell, consists in the guilt of Adam's first sin, the want of original righteousness, and the corruption of his whole nature – which is commonly called Original Sin; together with all transgression which proceed from it.'

(The Preface adds further that 'The Larger Catechism' was written in 1647 to make preparation for a common Church and Faith for the whole Kingdom; the project was never carried out and 'The Shorter Catechism' remains one of its few memorials.)

We are not told the purpose of the 'shorter' version other than that it was intended to prepare pupils to answer questions and it was assumed, with a touching innocence, that this little book contained full and unchangeable knowledge of all spiritual truth. In it there was no doubt but that unrepentant sinners would be consumed forever by liquid flames just as there was no doubt but that God had neatly produced the world in six days, resting on the seventh. Did we believe it? The answer must be 'yes and no'. Too many of our elders said it was true for us to discard it lightly: it was based solely on the Bible so it, of necessity therefore, had to contain Truth, and then 'no', we couldn't really believe all of it but were rather too awed, scared maybe, to sit down and, against the tide, worry it out alone. So, being the sensible creatures most children are, we closed our minds down to a fair degree when it came to things spiritual: God and his terrible wrath was for the Sabbath, and during the week we'd refresh our souls with the *Beano* and the *Dandy*.

We learned whole Psalms off by heart too, in a metrical version, and as these were all sung to good rousing Scottish tunes, I am often grateful for that because I can still sing them and carry much of that comforting book, 'The Psalter', around in my head, even today. Steeped in the Bible, we learned too of Israel's beleaguered history, about its prophets, priests and kings and these stories were as real to us as 'The Battle of Clontarf'; they were great yarns and easily captured our childish imagination – we loved Daniel and the lions' den, Joseph and his coat of many colours, and of course 'David and Goliath'. On top of all this, we also learned hymns off by heart and sang them too – hymns bent on giving us spiritual direction and discipline, mostly sung to the gayest of tunes. These too still find a place in my memory and when I hum out the words 'Awake my soul and with the sun …'e.g., I see all over again the full little church and the good suits and the best dresses bedecked further with little fresh posies picked in the garden on the way to church, and I hear again the eager thrum of voices lifted in praise of their Maker this sunny Sunday morn!

After Sunday School came church proper and set into the middle of this main morning service would be a children's mini-service with its own hymn, prayer and little sermon; this would be encapsulated then in the singing of psalms, of scripture paraphrases and of hymns, all sung lustily and gladly by the entire standing congregation for, above all, we loved to sing in church. Sandwiched between these musical outpourings were readings from scripture and long, long extempore prayers by the minister when we sometimes thought he'd forgotten us altogether, so rapt did he become.

Then came the sermon, which for Presbyterians was the *piece de resistance*; for this, people rearranged themselves into more comfortable positions: the organist would hoist herself off her stool, settle her fox-stole and slide into a seat in the choir; the man who pumped air into the organ to make it play would emerge from behind his blue curtain, and the occasional sweet or 'cough lozenger' would be slipped into mouths to help pass the next thirty minutes, for the sermon would indeed last that long and often longer. It was always based on a text from scripture and this text would be turned inside out and upside down, have its full meaning wrung from it in long meanderings, be illustrated by little anecdotes, its moral expounded and the consequences of ignoring that moral depicted in vivid language. Some people slept. I remember one young fellow who'd perhaps kept company with Bacchus the previous night, sleeping not only through the entire sermon but through all of the succeeding hymn as well while we, in delight, sang standing over him as he snored gently and alone in his pew. Most, however, stayed awake but all sighed when the minister finally came to the end of an exposition that had, no doubt, taken him a week to prepare. And no! incredibly, we didn't hate going to church! Not at all; and in the evening service which would be just as long as the earlier one, Sunday stretched itself lazily out in the red-carpeted warmth left over from the morning, and the oak pews, with their little brass holders for empty communion-glasses, were comforting havens.

That then, roughly, was mainstream Presbyterian religious indoctrination in the first half of the twentieth century in Ireland and, for all its sombre severity, I am forever grateful to it for the sturdy hand-hold it gave me on life.

The religious meeting we attended on Saturdays was a different affair altogether and was attended by children of all Protestant denominations; possibly it could be best described as 'evangelical'. I loathed this meeting with a passion – it was called 'The Class' – not least because it totally ruined my one free day, coming as it did exactly in the middle of the afternoon. It was conducted by a zealous lady, had a definite missionary thrust and its aim was to save our souls. As well as spoiling Saturdays, this class both nauseated and terrified me and often a fair bit of emotional blackmail was used to ensure our attendance, e.g. when the Circus paid its annual visit to town, we'd be asked to 'choose between the Lord and Duffy Bros' – a tricky decision to be thrust upon children and always we found ourselves in a no-win situation.

In National School, 'Religion' was just a bit of gas and it was really left to the church to fill the gap. When, in school, the time for 'Religion Lesson' came, the teacher simply retreated to his desk and papers, leaving us to ferret out ink-stained Bibles from a cobwebby press, to hunt for 'dirty' words in them with all our dirty, little-child glee; words like 'piss' we'd seize upon triumphantly, circle them loudly in ink and then write a note in the fly-leaf: 'See page 698' for future word-hunters. Sometimes a minister visited and gave a series of lessons; once, these consisted of interesting accounts of the adventures of Saul and David; once, we got a chance to learn some of the Church of Ireland catechism and the words just thrilled me with their poetry: '... keep my hands from picking and stealing and my tongue from evil-speaking, lying and slandering ...' and yet above all this, something else was stirring in my eight-year-old soul: something apparently unknown to either the Presbyterian Church or the 'Class' lady and something which I revealed to neither. This 'something' seemed to show me proof (and still does) that God really does exist and makes himself known not only in the world's orthodox, human approaches or its spiritual histrionics but away and beyond, independent in his Being, a loving God who casts a shadow here, stirs a leaf there, who broods over the entire cosmos with its beasts and humans, Buddhists and Presbyterians, tiny children and the people who just smile at the whole silly business! This 'indoctrination' from somewhere other than church or school came to me in another way and now I'll probably find that I have to change the tone of my language a bit to describe this.

Every summer, my parents rented a little house for a month on the shore at Laytown, Co Meath: the same house every single summer, the same stretch of sand in front of it so that gradually, it all came to seem as if it belonged to us and to us alone. We all felt at home there. Once, about four o'clock in the afternoon with the tide out miles, the way it does at Laytown, I followed it almost to its edge, crossing the wet, ribbed, greyish sand, barefoot. Completely alone, I knelt down and began to play one of my favourite games which was to dig out little subterranean, interconnecting tunnels, using razor-shells. I remember feeling very calm, happy, contented, fully-absorbed in what I was doing, listening to the dull scratch and grind of shell on sand. Occasionally my thoughts strayed to the bread-and-jam of teatime so I must also have been pleasantly hungry and then – how vivid it all is still – I was suddenly visited with and enfolded by an all-embracing sense of light, timelessness, universal knowledge and peace – me and everything else held together in silent, perfect unity. At that moment, I found myself in the presence of 'Something Other', something that didn't frighten, that made no demands: I can only call it 'God'. That 'visitation' lasted maybe two minutes at the most and I received it into my being as the most natural thing in the world, so much so that I didn't rush back up to the house to tell my mother or anyone else: there seemed no urgency, no need to. Then, for about twenty-five years, I don't believe I ever gave it a thought and I certainly never spoke to anyone about it and yet it stayed with me, deep in my being, to this very day, sustaining me in a way far more powerful than 'The Shorter Catechism' or 'The Class'. Because of it, I have simply been compelled to believe in God albeit sometimes angrily and reluctantly, and my later life, often turbulent and unruly and wild, always flowed from this secret spring which kept me, somehow, on the Way.

Years later when I lived in Montreal, I found it not just easy but natural to unite with Buddhists, Hindus, Muslims, Christians of all denominations as well as with renowned mystical visionaries such as Thoreau and Whitman.

So today, I often wonder about 'Religious Education' and the great fuss people make about passing on 'creeds' for I firmly believe that if none of it were taught, the Great Spirit, God, would himself find us out. And in an age when we lament that people lack religion and a moral sense, I think we should remember that we are not bigger than our Creator who is still, willy-nilly, very much in control although he often seems to be leading us along hard routes, leaving us to our own devices at times, even seeming to give up on us. But as long as the wind blows and the planets wheel in Time and Space, he is here. And isn't it a wondrous thing, I sometimes think, that while both church and state endeavoured to steer my own fragile boat into God knows what seas, it was really only the little wind of the Spirit that blew me home!

CHAPTER NINE

Hard Cash

In that thrifty home, money was seldom seen by us children although we knew it was somewhere in the air, like oxygen! It was in the rattle of the little till where pence and shillings were thrown in after the infrequent and small transactions in the shop. Sometimes we even managed to get a look into this till, a narrow mahogany drawer with a bell that didn't work and we'd look, but never touch, the flattened red 10/= notes in their own little compartment and alongside them, the prouder green ones. At the end of each long day, the till would be emptied, the 'takings' carefully counted and then transferred to the 'desk' to be locked away until they had accumulated sufficiently to warrant a visit to the bank. Visits to the bank were rare.

My parents didn't worship money nor did they hoard it but they did save it: it was saved for us, their children, so that we might be brought up decently, clothed and fed and educated to the best of their ability. That money was the fruit of their very hard labour and seen by them as a gift from God. Yet they were generous with what they had and my father in particular had no hesitation in helping out people who fell on hard times.

But to us children, it was an-out-of-reach magic: for you could get things with money, things like aniseed balls, as many as you wanted, and liquorice pipes and even more luxurious things like Mars bars and Cadbury's chocolate; you could even get a fairy-cycle like the one the Bank Manager's daughter had or a set of 'Children's Encyclopaedia' or a real Monopoly game (ours was home-made out of a sheet of cardboard with coloured paper strips for money).

But we just had to live with the fact that money we had none save for the occasional big, brown hen-penny given to us by a parent or a visiting relative whom we often shamelessly shadowed with greedy hope in our eyes. Tuesday, however, regardless of our penurious state, brought in the 'Beano' and the 'Dandy' without which I am sure I would have gone into a decline, young as I was. There were undoubtedly books aplenty in our house: the shelves bulged with great 'finds' always but the colourful comics that came once a week were things of rare bright beauty. Yet even these didn't relieve us of the weariness of forever being short of brown pennies, but still there was some sort of comfort in the knowledge that very few other children possessed these pennies either.

Given this state of affairs then, it is little wonder that when my sister Lucy found a half-crown on the stairs one day, time stopped. It was a perfectly ordinary day, a Wednesday afternoon to be precise when the shops were closed for the half-day and a gentle hush had fallen over the whole town. Our own shop was closed; our parents were busy in another part of the long, rambling house and our privacy was complete. Our friend Mabel and I crouched down in silent awe beside Lucy on the worn, carpeted tread. As we stared at what lay there, the sun beamed in on us through the fanlight over the hall-door and that dim stairway was lit up to make holy the big shiny silver coin with a horse on it! We knelt around it, not daring to touch, not even Lucy daring, whose 'find' it was. Then, at last she did pick it up and turned it over in her hand, turned it over in such a lavish, generous gesture that we felt wholly included, felt wholly equal participants in the 'find' so that, without demur or question, we three solemn children, one clutching a silver coin, wordlessly slipped out onto the deserted street that quiet afternoon. We had some money! And our hearts were beating fast!

On a half-day, there would be only one shop open, a tiny shop that usually sold nothing but hard little green apples, so what brought us here? Couldn't we have waited until tomorrow? Perhaps what caused the urgency was that my sister seemed miraculously to know that on this very day, behind the little hillock of green apples in the window, lay a totally unexpected consignment of Dutch chocolate. I had never heard of Dutch chocolate before but Lucy knew all kinds of interesting things, Mars bars and Cadbury's being the extent of my own knowledge. Anyway, we inevitably ended up with several thick bars of this exotic Dutch chocolate hidden up our jumpers. I don't remember how much it all cost but I think that Lucy was fairly profligate with that half-crown for I don't remember that we had any change for a rainy day. My conscience I quickly silenced even though I knew that a half-crown would buy a whole pound of butter or heel and sole several pairs of shoes.

Surreptitiously, we crept home and back to that very tread on the stairs where my sister had first spotted the treasure; and here, for it was surely a hallowed place, we knelt down and slowly, with something akin to sanctity, we broke and consumed the heavenly stuff without a thought for pounds of butter or the mending of shoes.

A few days later on yet another half-day, my sister found another half-crown in the same spot but we sensed no magic this time. Rational questioning took its place: where had this coin come from? Who had dropped it – was it the shop-boy hurrying out on a date – or even Marguerita, our eldest sister? But don't let's tell, we agreed, not yet anyway, and then away with us again for more of that Dutch chocolate which, to tell the truth was a little too bitter for my liking. But even as we again ate, we eyed Lucy accusingly; in response, she insisted that half-crowns just 'appeared' for her and sulked at our scepticism. In our hearts, she and I knew that my parents kept too tight a hold on their money, half-crowns, half-pennies and all, for any to elude their grasp and the Dutch chocolate tasted even more bitter still. Finally, our big brother John came upon us feasting among the golden wrappers and it was all over. Stern for his sixteen years, he demanded to know where the chocolate had come from and alas! there was none left to attempt bribery. Where, he demanded to know, had the amazing money come from with which to actually buy this chocolate. He threatened our silence with both father and mother until at last, Lucy began to babble confusedly about something that seemed totally unrelated to her 'miracle': she babbled about a cupboard in our parent's bedroom; she babbled about a little concertina-type cardboard mission-box (property of the Zenana Bible and Medical Mission) into which our mother occasionally and piously inserted a half-crown; she went on about squeezing and shaking this box until it yielded up its treasure, one piece this week, another next week.

Suddenly life was all flat and mundane: the glory of 'miracles' swept away leaving us in a state of sheer misery, with uncomfortable stomachs and guilty consciences and a dread of things to come. But Jack didn't tell on us and, as for my own conscience, I consoled myself that the black babies wouldn't have begrudged us those half-crowns; it was food and medicine they were said to need – not Dutch chocolate.

CHAPTER TEN

Teenagers

Although the word 'teenager' emerged into the English language as early as the seventeenth century, the particular species as it exists now at the beginning of the twenty first century had not yet unfolded itself, not even in the 50s: it hadn't even then begun to indicate that one day, out of that sluggish chrysalis of adolescence, would emerge a mammoth butterfly stranger than anything ever dreamt of – a creature of gargantuan proportions, beautiful, destructive, fragile; an unruly, turbulent being brimming with youth, flooded with sap; a being that would dye its hair at a whim from green to bronze to pink; that would dance to strange rhythms; tattoo its body and pierce its navel; use drugs and sex freely, first for pleasure and then to feed the pain of its addiction; that would make and spend money with abandon; demand and get its rights; banish all taboos and pretend to laugh at God while strangely filled at the same time with love for all God's children; that would make adults cower in a corner; a butterfly that would court death as it courted life.

That form of life was on the way though still very far off, and in the 50s things were still very different. No butterflies were we! Struggling out of childhood to grow through teenage years, we had much time to reflect on the misery of our condition and how sick we were of hearing the words, 'Now when I was your age …'

So, of course, we wondered what in fact it had been like in the first two decades of the twentieth century, especially for the women, and had to conclude that they simply must have had to batten down all instincts so that as soon as their young bodies cried out for the sun, they were quickly encased in long skirts, black sateen, buttoned boots and layers of complicated underwear. Like the bound feet of young Chinese girls, our mothers as teenagers must have been, at puberty, ritually forced into 'Little

Womanhood' for little women they suddenly became if all the sad portraits of youthful creatures enfolded in farthingales and wrappers are anything to go by. For them there was to be no more leaping of fences; their black-stockinged legs must be seen abroad no more; no more running; no more playground games; just a little of horse-riding side-saddle would be permitted (in Cavan they had only bicycles) along with home-making, the 'arts' and deportment and a patient waiting for a husband to turn up as he usually would in some form or other. This husband would not exactly be chosen for them but he would have to meet definite social standards. To remain single was a fate dreaded by all those women and, as children, we knew hardly a house but had its own usually eccentric 'Auntie' who had never married and who now lived in the home of a sister or brother; here she helped with the babies as they arrived, did housework, and all without payment or holidays. The few professions open to those early twentieth-century women included teaching and nursing; some rose to the heights of becoming cashiers or clerical workers in banks or Guinness's or the Civil Service; some gave piano-lessons; and all of these jobs had to be relinquished on marriage when the girl and her talents and her money, if she had any, became the property of her husband.

No! We were not like these girls who, when they in turn begat us and found 'teenagers' on their hands in the 50s and 60s, were quite hopelessly lost because even in those slow, snail-pacing times, society had changed, almost imperceptibly. Women's magazines had appeared and showed young ladies that there was more to life than buttoned boots and black bombazine. Make-up in attractive packaging became a regular feature in chemists' shops. Whalebone and steel gave way to elastic and the war was over, leaving in its wake such detritus as chewing-gum and nylons and all kinds of other American goodies for us life-trawling teenagers. And yet, as always with mothers, they really expected us to do more or less as they had done and, of course, became anxious and fretful when we didn't. Perhaps women can never learn that their daughters will never behave as they themselves did.

Be that as it may, as a thirteen-year-old girl, I and all my female peers were expected to leap into a murky, troubled land where we would learn furtiveness and deceit as a means of self-protection against adult wrath. We were expected happily to leave behind our playground of hop-scotch and marbles and leap-frog to enter a land, supposed to be adulthood or at least a path thereto but which seemed like something other for we were not regarded as adults yet, nor yet anymore as children. There was too a palpable feeling that society must, against all odds, contain us, lay hold on us, mould us. We felt we were a threat and yet we had no rights, no door-keys; we had few and limited freedoms. In that 'Land of Shades', we were expected somehow and automatically to come to terms with our emerging sexuality, our new 'moodiness', our sudden 'wildness' (for that's what they called it); expected to handle raging hormones that were as alive and active then as ever they were. And yet! what a profundity of silence surrounded us in those difficult times. No one at all spoke to us about sex.

I learned about menstruation from my mother while I'd my head in a basin having my hair washed and knew, sadly, that she was too embarrassed to look me in the eye while broaching the topic. Reproduction was never explained and we knew only what we saw in the behaviour of our farm-animals. The names of our body-parts we learned in a very genteel way from women's magazines, as even biology was not taught in the secondary school we attended. This new land of giddy excitement and haunting pleasure was also a region of shame and we knew not why. Menstruation was both a nuisance and an embarrassment: we were warned not to swim or wash our hair during a period and how well I recall the many furtive journeys to the kitchen range to destroy my 'shame', for the age of disposable materials had not yet arrived. Instead of handy tampons to be flushed away, we had to wear what were to us even then, horrid, fish-pink sanitary-belts to which the awkward sanitary-towel was fastened. But then, only a generation before that, our mothers had used rags which they had had to wash and rewash so, without realising it, we'd made just a little progress towards liberation!

Such was the fear and secrecy surrounding our adolescence, it was inevitable that hostilities should be incurred and this well before the term 'Generation Gap' had drifted across the Atlantic to our shores in the 60s. To have had even that flag to wave would, no doubt, have given us some sense of empowerment but we teenagers of the 60s had nothing, nothing beyond the wonderful places in our souls where dreams bred and light shimmered on the dewy cobwebs of the new dawn in us; where 'The Top Twenty' was like angels and violets and where we shared our glory-filled fantasies only with our sacred diaries, rust-marked from being kept beneath mattresses.

As for the sort of deliberate carefulness that developed between us and our elders, it was not seen as any logical development but something wilfully created by us rebellious and rather brazen young people who could be treated sometimes as children, sometimes as sixty-year-olds depending, it often seemed, on the whim of the adults.

So with stealth and cunning, with lies and deceit, we struggled painfully down the birth-canal to maturity. We couldn't talk about our dates because behind our dating always lurked the unspoken, maternal dread and shame of daughters 'getting into trouble' and the tone of my mother's voice didn't go unnoticed when she muttered that Mary Jane Cole had 'had a baby'. She made this birth sound the most horrible, evil thing but we never knew why although we fully realised, of course, that Mary Jane had, all by herself, been guilty of some heinous sin. On top of this, we were all most confusingly expected to date; it was almost a sacred duty to have a boy-friend and he had to be a Protestant boy at that for only when we were safely married to Protestants, be they ugly, diseased or, as was frequently the case, quite old, could mothers relax. Thus, girls tended to marry quite young and often, it seemed, to get a bit of peace! My own three sisters, Marguerita, Mildred and Lucy were all brides at twenty-one and mothers at twenty-three. A farmer proposed to me while I was still at school and I fled in terror at the idea of being so tied down; and for this, I came under my mother's wrath and scorn.

Incredible though it may hence seem, we led quite merry sex-lives. We were totally free from anxiety for we were wise enough then to understand what many of today's sexually active people don't, which is that sexual intercourse is not the only way to express physical desire. We fulfilled our urges in kisses and hugs and warm embraces; we learned each other's bodies without violating or being violated; we expressed our sex through all our senses: the touch of hands, the scent of cheap perfume that didn't mask the more erotic scents of our own bodies, the sound and sight of the beloved voice and face. That had to be enough for us since social taboos made us too scared to go further; beside we valued ourselves highly and openly despised anyone in our 'set' who 'played around' with the feelings of anyone else. On the whole we were happy and full of romance, singing it out by day and sometimes all night too when we stayed out under the stars and crept home at dawn as the birds awoke and the occasional donkey brayed, careful to avoid that creaking step on the stairs. We knew that we had done nothing shameful and so guilt never spoiled our dating; beside which, as a result, we never had to worry about sexually-transmitted disease or the AIDS virus. But, of course, some of us did get carried away, nature proving stronger than any taboo and, of course, babies were accidentally conceived, but in our group that was not the norm. When I think of all the girls I went to National School with, I can think of only three who, as the saying went 'had to get married' as if to make amends to society, somehow, for having transgressed its law. All of us would have been truly shocked at the idea of 'one-night-stands' and although contraception was, of course, available then (condoms for ages and ages), we had no reason to be really interested. I paint an idyllic picture to be sure, but even if it's only a half-truth in its subjectivity, it's my own truth for that's the precise way in which I and my friends knew sexual activity at sixteen-going-on-seventeen.

The 'better-off' teenagers amongst us went to boarding-school after National School or just stayed at home for further grooming; the less well-off went into domestic service. Because of my hard-working parents, all of my family went to boarding-school and here, life seemed, somehow, just to close down as we bent to the discipline of evening 'Prep' and crocodile walks, Latin grammar and love-notes slipped under the boys' dorm door.

But how well I remember the long summer holidays when, even then, we had to be home by nine o'clock on the loveliest of summer evenings – just in case! Holidays, when our sole entertainment (aside from the twice-a-month dance) was, for us girls just to walk arm-in-arm along the lovely country roads in the, usually vain, hope that our prince might have finished the hay-making or the threshing early and be coming to town in search of us. We smoked and we laughed. Oh Lord! how we laughed (probably the only real exercise we got come to think of it); and we told each other our stories, every detail spun out, enlarged upon and embroidered: what *he* said and what *she* said. Always, however, some deep-seated loyalty prevented us from scolding about our parents.

We knew every single person in our town and its adjacent townlands, knew every so-called 'character' and their 'wee ways'; we had a consummate interest in every aspect of every-body's lives, not just in our own age-group as tends to be the case today but in young and old, rich and poor; their speech-forms, their style of dress, their personal habits. We visited Cattie, the fortune-teller; gaped in fearful awe at bodies disfig-ured by accident or disease; loved the abodes of the dressmaker, the harness-maker, the cobbler and the watch-maker who worked in fetid gloom forever chanting, 'Watches and clocks. Watches and clocks,' as though he knew not another word. My sister Mildred went through a phase of being interested even in dead bodies and for a time visited every house where a corpse was laid out. We went to an occasional film in the flea-ridden cinema as well as to dances but there was no tennis or swim-ming and if we wanted to cycle, we had to, somewhere, borrow a bike for an hour while its owner, in from the country, did her shopping.

Nor was there such a thing then as 'holiday work' although we did, of course, work at home, but to be paid for this work was unheard of; indeed we never even thought in terms of pay-ment: that work was just another act of God like the weather. And one of the very worst of those summer-holiday jobs was to 'tramp' the hay! A cartload of good, dry hay would be piled up in King's Meadow, a mile outside the town and then come swaying into our yard, Joe the yardman at its head. Then he and another man would pitch it up into the yawning side of the loft while Lucy and I would be obliged to keep running over it, 'tramping' it as it was thrown up thus making still further room for more. It was hot up there as the hay rose higher and higher and the galvanised-iron roof seemed likely to burn us; the hay-dust choked us but no-one paid any attention to that; asthma was not then acknowledged as a threat and, in fact, was hardly known.

Another terrible bit of work was to bring in the cows for milk-ing and then drive them back again to pasture: we'd walk, Lucy and I, behind the four cows and four calves down the middle of the Main Street pretending not to be associated with them, terri-fied our boy-friends might be in town and see us. All would be well enough as the little herd swayed daintily onward until one of them would decide to urinate or worse in the street. Then they'd all stop and then, of course, Miss Posh from up the road, a taunt-ing young lady of our own age, would inevitably just happen to be passing and she'd nudge and laugh and we'd die of shame.

On wet days, my own secret heaven was in the hay-loft whence I'd take a ten-decker sandwich of buttered, plain bis-cuits and I'd nibble and cry over my novels, one of which, 'Mrs Haliburton's Troubles' by Mrs Henry Wood, was a favourite at the time. I swooned over Wordsworth and Keats and soulfully declaimed Hamlet's soliloquies through the open skylight in the attic that overlooked the slated roofs of the town.

It is hard to believe that I am writing of a time that was only about fifty years ago, but those were the days before TV, before man went to the moon, before CDs, before even the telephone had become an everyday bit of household apparatus. We our-selves hadn't even a gramophone then, although we had a little wireless-set that often emitted more crackles than anything else. Yet for us, they were good days and chiefly I remember how full of laughter they were, but we never guessed that for many other country teenagers in Ireland, life was little short of hell. We knew absolutely nothing about abuse or torture, rapes or killings; women's magazines never mentioned these things and we didn't scan the news columns of the papers where we might (but only *might*) have learned a bit more. Even natural death was re-mote from us at that time and we never stopped to think about the girls who'd 'had babies' or wondered what happened to them because these girls, few as they were, tended simply to dis-appear.

We believed the world was a good world made for ourselves to enjoy; it would go on forever; it wouldn't change. We believed firmly in God for there was never any reason not to; who, after all, but a god could have made our beautiful place and who but a god could turn a blind eye to our wildness? We knew beyond any doubt that we were in God's remit and that he himself was somehow a secret part of our very rumbustiousness.

CHAPTER ELEVEN

Family Wedding

It all happened quite quickly in the end. I mean my eldest sister's, Marguerita's, wedding, considering that for me the previous weeks had crawled. At eleven years of age, I was quite interested in 'weddings': they had so many facets – there was Fred, my new brother-in-law, to get used to; Fred was nice and funny with a huge rolling curl falling over his forehead; he read a lot of books, was quite stern and we had to mind our manners when he was around. Marguerita gave us filthy looks if we didn't, for she was very keen on manners too. Fred was only in his early twenties but we thought he was middle-aged. They were both at Trinity which place, it seemed to me, was something between a heavenly Temple and an extraordinarily difficult school. How almost fantastic then that these two lofty beings were now to be actually married!

And so there were the ongoing huddled conversations between my mother and the twenty-one-year-old Marguerita, for the latter was very soon to be a bride; there was the choosing of the bridesmaids who, it turned out, would be our Mildred and Molly Smith, Marguerita's best friend. There were also endless lists and so it was not to be wondered at that these lists sometimes got lost or misplaced and that my father was one day discovered wrapping up a pig-powder in the shop with nothing other than the guest-list.

There was also the bridal dress. Patterns were bought; dressmakers consulted; materials sampled and such was the angst that this dress caused that I dreamt one night that Marguerita walked up the aisle of our church clad in 'pink'; this dream caused me endless weeks of torment because it was said in the playground that to dream of a bride in 'pink', was to see her die before the day she plighted her troth; and firmly believing this, I watched my sister carefully for signs of decay until, at last something else distracted my morbid soul.

The 'something' was probably the guest-list itself for I do remember that this list (most often an abstract one) caused great disruption in our generally placid household: all the aunts and uncles would have to be invited and the first cousins and their spouses. But where did you go after that? What about second cousins? And their children? Indeed what about children at all? Old Mrs Thorpe would have to come for she had taught Marguerita her ABC ; also Mr and Mrs Puddock, for Mr Puddock had a fine repertoire of songs that would greatly entertain the guests. Then there was a whole lot of rather unimportant people who would be invited because they had some kind of tenuous link with our family – they couldn't exactly be classed as 'friends' or indeed as 'relatives' – they were just people who added some kind of pervading interest to our lives – these were the ones who wore two 'left' wellies when the 'right' one gave out, who chewed their food with their mouths open, who spat out their teeth by mistake when they laughed and whose mannerisms peculiar only to them amused and fascinated us. All of these my father would firmly call 'friend' and they simply had to be added to that guest-list.

When the guests were finally decided upon and the bridal dresses had been created in Misso Byrne's cunning little attic room by the sewing- machine that was operated by foot, our mother cast her eye on the rest of us, although I'd say it was Marguerita, not quite trusting my mother's dress-sense, who did most of the 'casting'! When I found myself togged out in a mustard-coloured coat and a matching hat like an army private's (or perhaps it was a little upturned boat), I didn't think too highly of the dress-sense of either of them but, of course, I could say nothing. Lucy was just as bad, maybe worse, for along with another mustardy coat, she was given a matching pork-pie hat with elastic under the chin. My brothers and father were easy: Sunday suits would do. Only my mother herself remained and she it was who was the greatest problem of all. Prior to this, I hadn't ever known that there was such a being as a 'Bride's Mother' but I began to learn! Nothing but the absolute best would do for her. Switzer's and Brown Thomas were visited and after she'd made endless trips to Dublin, arriving off the bus with huge brown parcels, we were at last allowed to behold the outfit. I thought it was grand but boring. I couldn't see why it had caused so much fuss, this nice, slatey-blue silk garment such as women of my mother's age wore, and the hat with the alarmingly wide rim that shook and rattled unexpectedly with beads and feathers.

Anyway, so far so good! The invitations, printed by the local printer and hand-written by Marguerita (even though she wasn't even the hostess), were all posted out. And now a new kind of waiting began for we knew that whoever got invited would have to give a present whether they wanted to or not – a right bit of trickery, I thought! Neither Marguerita not my mother was coarse enough to suggest that they might actually be waiting (in the deepest regions of their souls) for these presents to arrive but, almost surreptitiously, they did indeed begin desultorily to rearrange the furniture in the drawing-room. The sofa was pushed back against the wall along with the armchairs, and little spindly tables took up position in two rows down the centre of the room as if they too were waiting. Then, at last, the first present arrived! It was from Aunt Harriet. We all knew the writing. Marguerita peeled back the wrapping-paper not wanting to seem too vulgar by betraying eagerness. Inside was a little china tea-pot and a matching cup and saucer; there was a little card too with silver writing that said ' Wedding Bells!' and a fat little baby shooting arrows through two silvery hearts with the words: 'May your two hearts beat as one till all your days on earth are done.' I thought those were the most beautiful words I'd ever read and I pored over them again and again.

For weeks I watched in amazement as quite splendid gifts began to arrive, to be arranged proudly by my mother on every possible surface in the drawing-room. Marguerita was equally proud and amazed but too posh and snooty, I thought, to let anyone know it. So each gift was put on display with the inevitable silver and white card bearing the name of the donor, and you could, in the end, walk up and down little aisles viewing these offerings and feeling as if you were in a museum. There was a scallop-shaped butter-dish from Auntie Betty; an electric kettle from Cousin Joan; a teasing, sealed envelope from Uncle Jack with a card warning Marguerita 'not to spend it all in the one shop'; Mrs Quinn gave a knitted tea-cosy heavy with little woollen bobbles. In every case, all the donors of gifts, great and small, had their souls and purses bared in that room for it seemed as if the whole town came in just to have a look, whether they were invited guests or not. Once or twice, Lucy and I sneaked in some of our school friends and we scrutinised each gift, without touching of course, in an effort to make out the often indecipherable writing.

Then the day of the wedding actually arrived. I don't remember a single thing about the church service except that Marguerita really did wear pink and that Mildred, trailing behind the bride with Molly Smith, giggled a lot when she shouldn't have. After that, we were all ferried by hackney car (for we had then no car of our own) to a hotel seven miles away and there, it was all fuss and flowers and stout women in silk suits breathing out perfume. All extolled the bride's beauty and the groom's handsome bearing and I too thought what a nice person Fred was – so much nicer to me than my own brothers! He even let me hold his hand and I was very impressed by the fact that he carried brown kid gloves. When my mother had once asked Marguerita if she was really quite sure that she and Fred were suited, Marguerita was said to have replied with assurance, 'Oh yes! We speak the same language!' which my mother thought a very fine way of putting it, so much so that she aired this little story every chance she got.

After the 'wedding-breakfast' (funny title, I thought), the most boring speeches were made by important people but I'm sure my father didn't make any. And telegrams bearing good wishes were painstakingly read out and clapped at and even caused the odd teardrop to spill over. The photographer, who was also a guest, shuffled around the place with his gigantic camera, a fascinating thing with a huge black hood under which he disappeared occasionally, squeezed a big rubber bulb and then re-emerged to announce that a photo had been successfully taken. (We never did see those photos – family tradition has it that the photographer either lost or spoiled them or had simply forgotten put a film in his camera.)

Anyway, after the feast things livened up a bit although we all had to continue sitting at the table in our places: a family friend sang 'Coortin' in the Kitchen'; someone else said a recitation about a man called McBreen and his heifer and the minister, in his clerical frock-coat, made a happy, smiling speech looking much different from the way he looked on Sundays. The bride was toasted and so was the groom and all the other important people and I grew bored and wished for it all to be over.

Then at last they were off, Marguerita and Fred, away at 5 pm to catch a train that would take them to Kilkee for their honeymoon. Later we heard that Marguerita had cried on the train and I thought how silly she really could be underneath her grand ways. Cry on the train with Fred! Cry on the way to their honeymoon!

Back home, things felt flat. The drawing-room was rendered bare again save for its own stand-offish furniture: the gate-legged tables with circular brass tops, the three-piece suite and all the little spindly things. One other table, however, of a sturdier variety was introduced: this was a small, square mahogany table and on it stood now a big, brown cardboard box, tall and dark and deep, holding as it did the remains of Marguerita'a wedding-cake which was quite a lot of cake seeing as, originally, it had risen three storeys high: a big, big cake, a middle-sized cake and a very small cake (just like the three bears) all supported by delicate silver pillars. At the wedding-breakfast, only the little one and some of the middle-sized one had been consumed: the rest had come home, certainly not to be dined off by us who saw cake only at Christmas but to await the bride's return from her honeymoon. 'Then,' my mother explained, 'all the rest of the cake will be cut up in neat little slices and each slice posted to all those who'd given presents but who hadn't come to the wedding.' Little boxes to hold these slices were already stacked in a huge pile in the corner of the room; each was white and silver; each had address-lines on the lid and inside lay tiny, delicate, paper doyleys all ready for the little piece of cake to be inserted. These boxes of cake would be received with gratitude and solemnity and young maidens would place a little of it under their pillows in the hope of dreaming of their future husbands.

In the interval between the wedding and the end of the honeymoon, it happened that my brother Ernest spotted, one day, in the centre of the drawing-room's green carpet, a large, firm, white rosette, perfectly formed of royal icing. Now this to us was a 'find' indeed; a treasure to us who tasted such stuff but once a year, being content with 'curny' bread the rest of the time. At first, Ernest 'toed' the rosette with his shoe-cap, idly, fondly, and then, as Lucy and I looked on, he ate it. Outraged, we wondered where it had come from; Ernest winked towards the cardboard box on the square, mahogany table and then left, leaving us, his little sisters alone with temptation.

Of course, we succumbed! Stealthily, we lifted the lid of the musty-smelling box and gazed down into its depths at the thing that gleamed there white and magical. No harm could be done really! The wedding was well and truly over; my mother was back in the shop along with my father whose whistling we could faintly hear; Mildred was back in boarding-school and Jack was out somewhere. Marguerita was safe in Kilkee with Fred. Once again (as at so many other times in my life) there was only Lucy and me and, turning our heads aside as though to disclaim involvement, we dipped our hands into the darkness and seized on the hard whiteness, our fingers quickly breaking through to reach the dense, heavy, fruity stuff underneath. Then with our mouths full, and taking just a minute to reassure ourselves that, from where we stood, the cake looked just as nice as ever, we quietly moved away. Naturally one taste led to another and so it happened that, first on a daily basis, then by the hour (for we were two healthy children with normal appetites), we dipped and ate from the box always being careful to draw our chunks of the lush food from the very bottom and the very back where it couldn't be seen, not even – and perhaps especially – by ourselves!

Thus on the day of our newly-wed sister's arrival to cut up her cake into neat portions for the waiting boxes, we hardly felt a qualm: it was quite literally a case of the eye not seeing and the heart not grieving. Yet, we were *not* present when my mother, knife in hand and accompanied by her eldest daughter, rose to the last grand nuptial rite. We had hidden ourselves somewhere knowing we were doomed, too frightened now to imagine what they must say as they drew forth the poor collapsed thing with most of its hindermost and underparts in utter ruin.

I only remember that it was a Sunday morning and that, up in the attic, nursing our wounded souls in the piles of comforting dusty junk, Lucy and I decided that we must leave home, must run away from all the awful unkindnesses that we had been suddenly subjected to. We didn't feel innocent, mind you – we just felt that life had become simply too heavy for us. But of course, we didn't run away and, as far as I know, the cake was never mentioned again (maybe no one trusted themselves to mention it) and, to this day, I'm at a loss to know how they managed to find enough cake to post at all.

CHAPTER THIRTEEN

The Summer Holidays

Every morning in National School, the day began with our writing the day's date at the head of our copybooks. In this way, I grew to have an affinity with capital letters. The letter 'J' was my favourite for it introduced the summer holidays: beautiful, fresh June with its promises and then heavenly July with its sultry heat that fulfilled those promises and broke into gaiety and freedom around the middle of the month, releasing us all from our academic labours into bare feet and sandals.

Even before school ended, my mother began the holiday preparations. First of all, the two big, leather-covered trunks were hauled into a room which was called 'the nursery': the big, deep, chest-like trunk with its rounded, half-barrel lid and the tall, 'wardrobe-trunk' that stood upright and opened out to reveal a place for hanging clothes along with lots of little drawers that could be pulled open by their leather handles. Both trunks were green and we loved them as the symbols of our holidays, happily still to come. Then our mother would begin to pack them, a process that went on over a number of weeks and one that we inspected daily on our return from school. In the deep trunk, she put blankets and bed-linen, even pillows, and on top of these went sundry items that only she had the foresight to remember: bathing-togs and shoes and sometimes even broad beans from the garden. The 'wardrobe trunk' would hold all her own dresses and ours, boys' suits for Sundays and perhaps coats. The little drawers discreetly held all underwear. As well as these trunks, there was a small yellow, basket-case but I can't remember which of us owned this or what went into it specifically. My mother also ordered our transport, not that she really needed to for it was a well-established tradition in the town that we always went to Laytown in Co Meath on the 1st of August every single year in 'Brannigan's lorry and Petie Phair's car'!

72

The night before we set off was always too hot to sleep and Lucy and I, who shared a bed, tossed and turned endlessly longing for the new day, *the* day! And when it dawned, we were up and prancing around on the footpath, cupping our eyes melodramatically to see if the lorry was on its way yet from the bottom of the street, while my father and brothers struggled with the trunks. Then it came, the lorry, and in its wake, Petie Phair with his gingery moustache, majestic almost, in his car with the greenish windows. The trunks, and all the other equipment that had insidiously accumulated in spite of my mother's efforts to prevent it, were loaded onto the back of the lorry, and the biggest of us children, along with the maid, climbed in after them. My mother and Lucy and I, the two youngest, travelled in the car. As that lorry roared up the sleepy Main Street at 8 am, its passengers let out a great cheering and everyone was reminded that we were off. I envied my siblings their squealing from the lorry but felt happy enough to gaze out through the dim windows of the car and notice how it was that the hedges, and not the car, seemed to be in motion. Only my father remained at home to dispense medicines but he always joined us half way through the month.

The journey was usually without incident but a competition was always held to see who would see the sea first: the excitement of seeing it again was enough to make me feel faint – it was almost incredible that it should still be there from last year, that it should be as serene as ever, still rolling softly over the sands that we had churned up on our last holidays; incredible that the Mornington Tower should still stand and that the River Nanny still flow under the railway-bridge. The very air, smelling of sea and salt, was ours and awaited our arrival only; it was for us, and us only, that the wind sang in the wires to welcome us back as we fell out of lorry and car in front of the little house that seemed then no mere 'rented' house but our very own, a little house alive and breathless, with a past that gathered us all again into the present.

It was just a tiny house constructed of red galvanised iron, the end one of four fairly similar houses that stood in a row on a grassy bank overhanging the shore. Ours had a porch with white, wooden lattice-work at the front and, inside, a seat on either side and then the front door itself – a simple little brown, wooden door without letter-box or knocker. In the house, there was a kitchen with a range, two bedrooms and a sittingroom (which we always used as a bedroom) and that was all; every room with its dark-brown wainscoting, was fully taken up with beds (and beds alone) and had its own washstand with ewer and basin; the lavatory was outside, round the back. In front was what we called 'the plot': a tufty, grassy piece of ground where we could slide down slopes or sometimes sit and read a book if we had time, but I think 'the plot' was used mostly by adults and, incredibly, some of these did come to stay: aunts and cousins and even our friend Mrs Smith when she could be per-suaded to leave her farm. I have no idea where we all slept: seven of ourselves (eight when my father arrived), the maid and then the guests – perhaps we children slept three or four to a bed. But the greatest and most joyous fact at the beginning of our holiday was that we'd stay here for one whole month, what-ever the weather!

The arrival of my father was always a big event. Already one or two of us would have let him know, by post, that we needed a little money, and one time Mildred sent him a card that he trea-sured because it so amused him: it was a typical seasidey card with fat ladies and men with bulbous noses and a rhyme that went: 'Everything's dear, dining and beer; bathing and boating, send me some notes.' We were never sure how he actually made the journey to Laytown but he always arrived in exactly the same way: just walking across the strand from Bettystown, and on the morning of his arrival, we'd stand for hours on the look-out for our big, laughing father who would be clad now in just a shirt and the flannel trousers (held up partly by string) and sporting the white tennis-shoes kept especially for Laytown. When he appeared, we'd run to meet him as if he'd been away for years.

During that month, we went barefoot and spent our time outdoors except when it rained just too heavily, and then we played cards, sprawled out over the beds in a bedroom, but mostly we were outside. We started our days around 6 am be-cause even on holiday my mother kept to 8 pm bedtime – proba-bly she had had all she could take of us by that time. We played on the strand and we 'swam' which really meant that we all did the 'dog-paddle' with our landlubbers' hands firmly on the sea-bed. Our swimwear was very unsophisticated and I remember that my own outfit, at one time, was made of a hairy, orange material that felt like wool. One winter, my mother spent the dark hours knitting a huge garment for herself to swim in and the construction of this was quite a feat in itself: it was in one piece, had a knickers-bit under a skirt which ended in a woolly ruff and the whole of the upper piece was done in a sort of checker-board design; on each shoulder was a button and a button-hole. It was a unisex outfit for whenever my mother wore it, she did so with both shoulders securely fastened; when my father wore it, he took his 'dip' with the button on one shoulder open. That garment never got a chance to dry out (no more than our own) for we were in the sea every single day, besides which it was so heavy with sea-water that drying it would have been impossible, and it is hard now to think that putting on wet, rough outfits to go swimming was fun – but it was. That huge garment, manufactured out of odds and ends by my thrifty mother, never appeared a second summer. I think it must have shrunk so badly that she didn't even dare suggest that one of us should wear it, as would have been like her.

On the days when we were given a penny, we went over to the shop, our favourite of the three. Mr Sharpe was there always, inside this lovely, sweet-smelling place with its scents of fresh bread (stored under upholstered seats each side of the door), scents of ice-cream and, of course, sea. We had travelled 100 miles to get here from Cavan, we told him, (really believing we had) and then proceeded to order his speciality: 'Mickey Mugs'. These were absolutely delicious confections. A 'Mickey Mug' consisted of coloured and flavoured water frozen solid into an egg-cup so that we had to spend a very long time scraping it out; for that reason, he always let us bring the egg-cup home and return it later when empty. They cost a penny each – maybe to cover the risk of the egg-cups! He was a clever, friendly man who seemed to like children a lot for he always tried to please us – for example, he'd find potatoes in funny shapes and use them to make characters which he'd then display in his window for our delight.

Across from this shop was Mr Ryan's. Mr Ryan was much less approachable than Mr Sharpe but his shop was divine and dark and full of sweets and toys and gewgaws. I remember once buying a little yellow bird there: it had 'real' feathers and sang, and flew off and round and back again when I twirled the end of its stick.

Nearer our house was the Tea-Shop, a dull enough place selling as it did only tea, but in the field next to it was a 'summer-house' and this was of great interest. It was a green, wooden structure divided into four compartments and it could be turned around and around on a kind of mobile platform so that no matter where the sun was, one could always sit in its light. One lady did sit in it often and she was an 'invalid' or at least we said she was, for who else in their right minds would want to sit in a summer-house all day? And sometimes we gave her a little 'spin' in that summer-house: two or three of us tugging and hauling (on the other side of her where she couldn't see us), would gently and very slowly twirl her about; we thought we were being very 'bold' but she always smiled and sometimes laughed when we did this but it spoiled our game which, to be any fun, required that we run away, in mock-terror, at the end.

Further down was a butcher's and grocery, two pubs and a post-office and that was all. There was no chemist's, no hairdresser, no dentist and I doubt if there was a doctor. The post was delivered by a post-girl and the milk by a milkman who poured what we needed out of his measuring cans directly into our jug. Peter Lyons himself brought the bread in his horse-drawn cart – at least I always thought that it was Peter Lyons and I always looked at him in admiration and thought how proud he must feel about winning all those medals that his cart said he'd won.

Sometimes we went to play in the railway station which was a quiet but interesting place; trains sometimes passed through on their way to Dublin or Dundalk, passenger trains and 'goods' and we always stopped whatever we were doing to count the carriages which usually were far more than in these days of road-travel. Standing on the downside-platform, we'd watch the black, puffing engine nose its way around the bend and into the station; passenger trains always stopped; 'goods' always flew through and often, we'd rush up onto the little footbridge and stand, clinging to each other as the train roared beneath us often leaving us with black smuts on our clothes or, worse, in our eyes. We played our games in the two waiting-rooms and eyed greedily the little chocolate-bars in the machine; we visited the signal-box and we performed climbing stunts on the iron-work that undergirded the footbridge. Sometimes the Station Master came out from his imposing yellow-brick house to tell us to go away and always rejected our plea that we were expecting 'our auntie off a train' – it never occurred to us that he might be privy to the knowledge that another train wasn't due for several hours.

Sundays happened in Laytown too but even they became magical here. Sometimes we children were sent on our own to the Church of Ireland church in Julianstown, walking four miles each way. This church was a real treat to us Presbyterians with its stained glass and beautiful Communion Table. We were always greeted with smiles by people at the door and given strange books to use in the service, during which we had to control our giggles for we never managed to discover at which points we were supposed to sit or stand or kneel – we never really knew which. When we didn't go to this church, we went instead in the evening to the Schoolhouse and going here was pure delight! First it meant a stroll over Laytown's road (it was not a 'street') at the end of which we entered on a mud-packed pathway that wound around some mussel-beds and took us to the Nanny Bridge. This little bridge, with its wooden planks and iron railing, spanned the river almost exactly under the railway-bridge (but not quite) so that we could stop and peer into the swirling water beneath us or look up into the great red, metal pillars and girders that supported trains. The river was full of crabs that went about their lazy business in the giant seaweed-fronds, and when we reached the end of the bridge, we were in front of a couple of lovely, little rose-covered cottages and then just ahead was the Schoolhouse. I think some of the charm of the Schoolhouse must have lain in its very name. It probably was a school in the winter or may, at one time, actually have been a school. In any case, it was a lovely, little building with a real bell that actually rang out. Here too, the service (for it was used as a church in the summer) was Church of Ireland and when it was over (always pleasingly short) we had that glorious return journey home to look forward to.

On one day in the month, Mildred took myself and Lucy on a trip to Drogheda. This day was a real highlight for we made the five-mile journey by train. It was absolutely wonderful: just to stand on the platform with Mildred who clutched both us and the tickets tightly and then, when the train pulled up, to enter the carriage of our choice (they always seemed to be empty) and sit facing each other on the long, plush seats. Mildred never let us move around too much: she kept us away from the doors on each side of the carriage, wouldn't let us put our heads out in case we got smuts from the engine in our eyes, wouldn't even let us fiddle with the big leather straps that were meant for opening and closing the windows. That little train made strange and lovely music for us Cavan children as it chuffed and shuddered and jolted along the shiny track. Then to arrive in Drogheda! And what a wonderful town that was. So much bigger than our own at home and yet not as big or frightening as Dublin. Mildred always took us first to the Mooreland Café for buns and a drink. Then we'd go the 'Wee Woman' who, according to my father, sold the best sausages in the world, and then we'd go back home by train to Laytown delighted to have had such a splendid day. And that's exactly all I remember ever doing in Drogheda and yet, because of these simple things, I have always loved that town.

Often during this holiday month, we set out for the day at the crack of dawn. The world was so free and so safe then that we didn't have to tell our parents where we were going or when we'd be back: for we never *knew* what time we'd be back, not having a watch between us. And time, quite literally, meant nothing to us. We might wander over the strand to Mornington and play at the Tower there, coming back through Bettystown by a road that wound through fields yellow with ripe oats or wheat. Sometimes we went the other direction and headed for Mosney to spend aeons of time in its woods and its dunes; the 'Holiday Camp' had not yet made its appearance and the place was empty except for ourselves and the rabbits. There was just one caravan and this belonged to the rector of Julianstown

Church of Ireland church, the place where, we presumed, he spent his own summer holidays. The rest was ours alone and very often during those timeless days, I'd find myself pausing briefly just to be aware, to be conscious of the glory of it all and to wonder idly if I had had my dinner already – or was that yesterday? For those days were without the normal parameters of mealtimes, which seemed to occur just when and if we were hungry.

What a paradise my mother created for us and how on earth did she cope and manage not to spoil our freedom by imposing regulations to assuage her own need to protect us from life. She gave this to all of her children so that, even today, all six of us return at times to Laytown, alone and on secret pilgrimage, to pay homage to the place that gave us 'the pearl of great price'. The little house is gone but, thankfully, a small picnic area with a wooden table has been put on the site so that we can sit there and look at the exact same stretch of sand where once we played.

When August drew to a close (and we never spoiled it by gloomily reflecting on how few days were left), we packed up smartly and returned to Cavan. I don't remember the journey home but I do remember being told that I'd be back at school the very next day and that was always a terrible shock. Sometimes we tried to prolong the holiday in our imaginations: we'd fill the bath at home with cold water and get out the orange togs and we'd hang up the length of seaweed that was supposed to tell us when rain was due and we'd listen to the sea singing from a shell held to our ears – but it was no good! – Laytown wouldn't be back until next August.

CHAPTER THIRTEEN

Orange?

People outside the province of Ulster may find the mind-set of those Ulster Presbyterians who live south of the Border a little quaint, a little difficult to understand. It is very easy to forget that they are quite literally of different stock. They are Ulster people who are citizens of the Irish Republic. Their ancestors are Scottish (maybe that's where they get their canniness from) and they'd have cheered King Billy on. They'd also have defended Derry's walls along with the Apprentice Boys and they are still my people; I am still of them; I will share their psyche always, however hazily.

In the decades that I write of, however, their 'Orangeism' had become a little anaemic since they had long since had to incorporate themselves into an Irish culture that could still feel strange at times, a culture dominated by the Roman Catholic Church and Irish Nationalism, both so secure in their positions in society that they could afford to give minorities trivial little licences here and there. But the exercise of their Presbyterianism was no trivial licence to these Ulster people south of the Border; their religion was something they'd never willingly abandon; they'd paid too great a price for it in the past; sadly, however, Rome's *Ne Temere* decree sometimes did force them to 'turn'. But when it came to Orangeism, well that was an entirely different matter! To be Orange was an optional extra, a frivolous frill that threw a blade of colour onto otherwise dull lives in July and August and it was quite unlike what was experienced in the Six Counties.

When I was a child in Cavan in the 40s, it was the normal thing to have one's whole family connected to the Orange Order. But my own parents were, strangely, not members; my father, in particular was opposed to Orders of any kind and I guess that my mother may have thought them beneath her. But my brother John belonged to a local 'Lodge' and sometimes, in the mood for flaunting his new manhood, he'd show us his sash, taking it reverently out of the bottom drawer of his battered wardrobe while we huddled around him in awe at first. He must have found us a rather disappointing audience in the end, Lucy and me, for we were never very impressed by the reality of the faded-looking scarf with funny little symbols stitched onto it.

Every summer, Orange Services were held in our own church with our neighbours and relatives proudly parading up the aisle, men and women together, from the grounds outside right up to the front pews. One hymn that was invariably sung was 'Onward Christian Soldiers, marching as to war' and this hymn with its bellicose words and rousing tune always made me throw my shoulders back, although I had no notion of what war I was supposed to be marching to, other than that it seemed to have something to do with the menacing Roman Church.

In the privacy of our own small 'place of worship', we could let off steam, admire the black bowlers, the banners and sashes, while indulging in such hymn singing as might be expected from a withering population that felt itself beleaguered – as indeed it really was. It must be remembered, however, that Ian Paisley hadn't yet been heard of in Cavan; his besmirching of our Presbyterianism still had to come, and it must further be remembered that his so-called and self-initiated 'Free Presbyterianism' had nothing to do with my mainstream Presbyterian Church – nothing at all.

The LOLs (Loyal Orange Lodges) were dotted around the countryside – humble little one-storey buildings that often looked no more impressive than well-kept sheds, and over the door of each was a little concrete slab declaring its title: 'Billyhill LOL'; 'Lisdonnan LOL'; Lisball, Breakey, Stonewall, Drumbeg etc. There seemed to be one in every townland, none in the town itself, and if this had any significance, as it must have, we didn't know about it. During the winter, these buildings were probably just used for members' meetings but, coming up to the summer, they sprang alive: doors were thrown open, sashes brushed, flutes burnished and drums dusted down for there would be a lot of practice to be done by the bands if they were to perform well on the 'Glorious Twelfth' which, in reality, meant about as much to us as children as a Fair Day!

To give them their due, Roman Catholics never interfered with these celebrations, no more than we interfered with theirs. They probably saw our Orange antics as being frivolous and silly, just as we smiled at their Corpus Christi processions. Without hesitation, we could announce to all and sundry that we were going to a 'Walk' on the Twelfth – very often in the North itself – and an indication of how acceptable all this was lies in my once suggesting to Ernest that he should dress the shop-window especially for the occasion, that he should fill it with boxes of Kleenex, and a placard that would read, 'If you can't beat the Big Drum, you can blow your own trumpet with Kleenex!' My brother refused to adopt the idea but if he had, I don't believe a soul in the town would have minded. Anyway, in those days in Cavan, no stones were thrown, no windows broken, no one hurt. There was just no ugly feeling that I was aware of (although I remember, on one occasion, deeply resenting being told that I wasn't Irish because I was a Protestant) and, of course, it was quite beyond our comprehension that there might be deeper, more dangerous currents which, one day, when religion of any kind was all but swamped, would erupt into a cruel, death-bearing deluge. And yet, most probably, our parents who had known the Black and Tans and Civil War, comprehended more than we could guess.

With regard to our place in society, it had often seemed to me that Roman Catholics in the Republic saw us Protestants as not only a distinct but as a slightly superior class which, if that were really the case, puzzled me. Protestants had to be admired for their confidence: what woman, for example, but a Church of Ireland rector's wife would have the nerve to plough into our shop on a Fair day in her wellies and demand, right behind the counter, to see my father about her horse which had 'the botts'? It was perceived further that Protestants were hardier, thriftier, tidier; they even seemed to live longer! They also had to be pandered to, their complaints taken seriously by those in 'high places' lest the State be accused of repression. The Protestant ways and accents were seen as being still fairly representative of a vanished 'ascendancy', an ascendancy despised by us Presbyterians who had never been included in it at the best of times and who had, on occasion, been soundly abused by it.

Protestants (remember that 'Protestant' meant all Christians who were not Roman Catholic) were seen to be better educated and went to boarding schools, a habit often misunderstood for we went to such schools in an effort to preserve our culture and ethos. Presbyterians, however, were not a swanky lot nor indeed were we generally well-spoken: we used the local dialect; we talked about getting 'japped' (splashed by rain or by fat from the pan); we talked about not doing a 'hate' (a thing); about sheughs and gasons; we said 'kyap' for 'cap' and 'Hugh' we pronounced as 'Q'. The more uppity Protestants, in our minds, tended to be members of the Church of Ireland and they went to posh boarding schools like Alexandra College or St Columba's. Nor were we in Cavan like those Dublin and Cork Presbyterians – we were true culchies and felt so utterly inferior to those people in the east of the country who could say the word 'actually' with closed eyes and British-sounding drawl; it was only when we went to university that we learned to be objective and to laugh at ourselves.

But to return to Orangeism and its espousal in Cavan, it was all just about making music with pipe-bands and having wild hooleys in the countryside – that was all! Once, a Church of Ireland clergyman banned Orange Services from his church in our town. Perhaps he thought that Orangeism in Cavan was truly about loyalty to a foreign power whereas, in fact, it was nothing of the kind. Cavan people are renowned for their 'cuteness' and it would have taken the Grand Master all the way from Belfast to divine how really uncommitted we were to his cause. We were more Green than Orange, more closely bound to Dublin than to Belfast, more at home with Cavan Catholics than with fellow-Protestants in Dublin's salubrious suburbs. We were just Cavan people and the Cavan Catholics accepted us as we were, in spite of the vagaries of the Glorious Twelfth and in spite of the fact that deep in our collective psyche was still a link, however tenuous, with Northern Ireland. Of course, it was a struggle to hold on to our Presbyterian identity against mighty odds but aside from the *Ne Temere* stranglehold of the Roman Church, we were freely allowed to do this in whatever way we chose.

CHAPTER FOURTEEN

The Back Yard

Although we lived in a town, my parents kept a limited but varied number of creatures in our long, narrow backyard with its lofts and stables and byres. This, no doubt, would have had a lot to do with the fact that both of them had been reared on farms and indeed I remember my mother, in a rare outpouring of feeling, telling me how she had wept in that yard as a new bride, finding herself surrounded by walls and sheds and the roofs of other houses beyond them. But also, both my parents had an acute sense of being blessed by a Divine Loan, a loan that, no matter its guise, must be used and used well like the biblical talent and passed on to the next generation in even better condition than they'd received it. So their byres and nesting-boxes and stables just had to be filled and employed just as they themselves had to be employed, as we children had to be employed and all, implicitly, to the greater glory of God whose name was rarely actually heard in our house (certainly never in swearing) but whose presence was most mightily felt.

God was not only in the 'Burning Bush' – *Ardens sed Virens* (burning but not consumed, the Presbyterian motto) – he was everywhere in our lives, and so by a straggly extension of this philosophy, we drank milk (unpasteurised) from our own cows, ate the eggs of our own hens, our own pork, and our own bread and butter, both of these being made by my mother. We raised our own Christmas birds and, of course, grew all our own vegetables. Not a thing was wasted nor was a minute of our precious time; and how clearly I recall, for example, the hours spent on my knees as a child in hilly, wet fields, thinning turnips and being stung by nettles in the process.

Over our mini-farmyard hung the cobwebs of Old Testament times and indeed of the New as well, for we hadn't then yet learned that animals were God's creatures just as we ourselves were. We understood only that animals had been created for man's benefit and were there, solely, for us to use for our own good, since we still reckoned ourselves to be the Supreme Creation. So when we killed with our traps and our axes, often in unintentionally very cruel ways, we saw this as 'Nature red in tooth and claw' which seemed quite just, and we accepted that our own turn to be 'bloodied' would eventually come too in some way or other in the very order of things.

So our relationship with our animals was arrogant and benign, intimate but ruthless. Spiders, earwigs, woodlice, mice and rats shared our house; cats, dogs, pigs, cattle and fowl shared our yard. We had fleas too but not head-lice (my mother dealt with the latter with smelly pomades and steel-toothed combs) and we coped happily with all. We never used pesticides (probably there were none to use) and summer after summer in our kitchen and scullery hung long sticky, dirty-looking fly-papers covered with the bodies of dead flies. Fleas we caught with pieces of soap and only in great emergencies (and there were not a few!) was a bit of strychnine-charged bait laid for a rat.

So even as town children, we had the fullness of life and of death in our own backyard in the form of dumb creatures mostly loved even if in a rather high-handed manner. We knew that a pig's skin felt cool and rough, a cow's coat fine and feathery. We knew too about the ungentle business of dehorning animals, of castration, of bringing cows 'to the bull' and of cutting puppies' tails. Yet our animals were never hurt sadistically and I think we tried in our own crude ways to be gentle, even in the infliction of what we saw as inescapable suffering.

In that yard was a sow betimes, and pigs almost always, and when these pigs were big enough, we children played a 'wild-west' game with them right in their sty: one of us would try to clamber onto the animal's back while the others sat on a wall and cheered us on in what we thought was 'Rodeo' style. The pigs always won out – they were too strong for us. (In those days no one that we knew of, or at least cared about, fussed about getting dirty with manure, and I don't remember that we did much in the line of hand-washing – still, we were never sick.)

Sometimes a day would come when a pig, perhaps the very

pig we'd played with, had to be killed and I confess we felt no sense of grief whatsoever. Instead we'd remove ourselves to a safe distance and watch as much of the entire proceedings as we could with the insatiable curiosity and indeed barbarism that is found, but generally repressed, in children. It sickens me now, however, when at last those blocked feelings of revulsion have floated to the top of my mind like ugly oil-slicks, to recall the two lean peak-capped men in shirt-sleeves and their murderous, blunt weapons and, in a corner, all by itself the lone pig. I hear, in outrage now, the dying animal's screams that filled us children with terror and also I see how, later on, the dead, white thing, sad-looking and totally defeated, was hung by its hind legs from the rafters in the turf-shed with new rope. We'd watch the gutting and the scraping and the final 'salting' taking place at the back door when the pig, now in handy briny parcels would be packed away in tea-chests in our dairy as food for the coming year. My mother always made brawn from the head, a delicacy I never fancied, but I can't remember our ever eating the feet.

We had cows too and bullocks and calves, all kept out on pasture but occasionally we'd have a cow due to calve and this one would spend her time quietly waiting in the warm byre. Joe, the yardman, along with my father or a brother always sat up that night and in the morning, before we went to school, we'd run down to see the new, wet, staggery little creature: the bawling cow's miracle. Once or twice, I witnessed the amazing birth itself, a sight that always left me speechless with wonder.

As well as a couple of dogs, we had thirteen cats, mostly stripy creatures of indefinite breed but Hans, the big, black one with the white medal on his chest must have been their king. He was a beautiful animal and when we picked him up, he'd an endearing habit of wrapping his two front legs around our necks. 'Hans!' chuckled the local Rector, 'They call him Hans and him all feet!' We despised that joke. Once, Lucy had the idea of organising a Cats' Home in the loft, and painstakingly we made thirteen beds in boxes with the name of each cat printed on every box, but when not even the intelligent Hans agreed to cooperate and the other animals were still less compliant, we abandoned the project leaving them to rummage through their own murky but preferred places.

Then there was 'The Rat'! – 'Mister Rat' we called him because, while rats did indeed frequently enter our house to be
eventually trapped or chased outside by my mother, Mister Rat
seemed apart and untouchable in the glory of his splendid ability
to survive against heavy odds. At night, as we lay in bed, we'd
hear him and we'd know who it was because Mister Rat had a
limp, possibly as a result of a close shave with a trap. Over the
ceiling above our beds, he'd scamper slowly but gallantly on his
nocturnal business and, in spite of all her best efforts, my mother,
the Rat-Catcher Supreme, never managed to catch him. He presented a huge challenge to her but, in the end, I think he must
just have grown old and, like the old soldier, faded away.

We had a donkey called Maisie and numerous fowl. Hens
laid lovely warm, dirty eggs in their nesting-boxes in the hen-
house. There were 'clocking-hens' too in partly-covered tea-
chests with a brick on the top of the lid; these birds warmed and
guarded their clutch of eggs until that very exciting day when
the tiny, damp yellow chicks began to peck their way out of the
shells. We kept ducks and sometimes we had geese and a gan-
der that always seemed cross; coming up to Christmas, there'd
be a few turkeys. Of all these birds, I think it was the baby ducks
that I loved best: lovely little downy things with such intelligent
eyes like polished seeds, waggling their impertinent bodies
through the yard. Once my brother John, when he was very tiny
himself, tried to hasten the ducklings' progress by teaching
them to swim in the tub of water under the pump: sadly, he
drowned them all. It was only the dogs and the cats, however,
that we were encouraged to grow attached to – the rest were all
simply 'in transit'.

Easy days. Easy ways. I don't think my own daughter would
have had the chance to handle more than a dog or a cat – certainly
never a duck or a pig. Things have changed and in that same
town today, people would no longer take it lightly to be splat-
tered with fresh cow-dung by a passing beast or to step unwittingly into a pile of sheep's 'pills' on the footpath. We've become
much 'cleaner', more worried about hygiene and overall, I think,
less healthy. We eat too many antibiotics and other things that
we either didn't have or couldn't afford in those times. How
people today might shudder to know that, as children, we often

sat down by the 'dunkill' (a place where ashes, refuse and dung was all indiscriminately dumped) and deliberately cut little nicks in our legs or forearms with pieces of broken delph – just so that we could run up to the shop and 'win' a strip of sticking-plaster!

But in one respect, at least, does my home town still carry the banner of earthiness: it has never yet to this day, as far as I know, got more than a mention in a Tidy Towns Competition and, per-versely, I find this fact pleasing.

As for 'yards' like ours, I doubt if there is even one left and if there is, there are no creatures living there. I imagine that prop-erty developers see all those yards (and every house on the Main Street had one) as a potential place to construct flats to house the people who insist on commuting to their work in Dublin.

CHAPTER FIFTEEN

Julia

Julia was one of a long line of maids in our house and, like the others, lived in the attic. To reach the attic, you went up the carpeted stairs and then the lino ones until at last you got to the bare boards where wallpaper gave way to paint and, finally, to whitewash.

Perhaps the most majestic thing about the young Julia was her name conjuring up, as it did, images of heavy Caesars, for she was very fat, obese you might say, and even when doing housework (of which she did only a little), she always wore a loose, grey garment that flowed about her, a cross between a housecoat and an overall. This garment covered even her apron which perhaps was just as well, for various reasons. In addition to being stout, Julia had an extraordinarily agreeable and placid nature; her red face forever glistened in a damp smile even when Joe teased her about 'piping in the haggis' as she'd waddle into the dining-room with the 'joint' for Sunday dinner.

Sometimes, when we were small, she invited us to visit her in her attic and these visits were precious to us because they were in strange territory, albeit in our own house, and often yielded up the esoteric. Up there, in the dust of forgotten glories, was the dark, windowless room where the bogey-man lived, and then the larger L-shaped place filled with discarded fans and feathers, beaded screens and a battered pram made for the twin babies, only one of whom, Marguerita, had lived.

Then there was Julia's room. It had a little crooked, wooden door that seemed to hang in mid-air; we certainly could have squeezed under it at a pinch but Julia always solemnly opened and closed it using the iron latch. Inside was a slanting floor of well-worn, unvarnished boards, white-washed walls and very little furniture. In fact, as I remember it, there was just a narrow iron bed covered with multi-coloured spreads and worn-out patchwork quilts, a chair, and beside the bed a little table for her candlestick and the fearsome-looking alarm clock with double bells on top, that most essential of a maid's possessions. Behind a curtain hung her few personal garments. And that was all. From the skylight, her only window, could be seen about a foot of sky and distant hills, but mostly the view consisted of sturdy acres of slated roofs that shielded the wealthy citizens of our town.

In summer, this room would be unbearably hot and the skylight would be kept open and the little door would swing crookedly off its latch. In winter, it was the opposite, making it necessary for Julia to warm her bed with a brick heated in the oven, and often I guiltily thought of her up there in the cold, flickering dark, getting into bed beside her brick and then blowing out the candle in its chipped, blue, enamel holder – for 'the electric' hadn't been taken as far as the attic.

When we visited her in her room, she would receive us with gracious hospitality. She'd let us sit on the bed, Lucy and me, and together the three of us would pore over her treasures spread so generously before us – a pearly brooch and a bottle of scent with carnations on the label, a set of silver buttons, stray shoe-buckles and a little calendar with a picture of a curly sailor-boy in blue trousers. These were kept in a box under the bed. But on the bedside-table, beside clock and candle, was a greenish-yellow bottle containing what she called 'Holy Water' and a string of tiny, rattly, black beads with a cross and a figure of Jesus attached to it; these, she explained, were her 'rosary beads' but she could never make us understand why these beads were so precious to her, why she never wore them or what they were actually *for*. Her best treasure of all would come last. She'd hold the red-edged, little black book to her heavy bosom and say, almost teasingly, 'Now! Do yous want to see God?' and to us Presbyterians, who were allowed neither image nor sign of the Holy One, this question would amount to total blasphemy, to serious profanity! And then, 'Oh, yes, we do!' we'd breathe. So, fumbling in her book, she'd produce his picture, head only, but God indeed, a sad and sickly God with upturned eyes and crown of thorns and we knew we'd never tell what we had seen in Julia's attic.

That was when we were small. Only when we began our-selves to grow did we realise that most nights Julia in fact disap-peared. When she'd finish her day's work around 7 o'clock, she'd spend some little time in her attic room and then be gone, gone so silently, so swiftly, that no one ever saw her go and certainly no one ever saw her come back, as it would be in the darkest hours, and after who knew what adventures, that she'd return. She intrigued us and would never tell us where she went or what she did. 'I keep myself to myself', she'd say, an expres-sion that sounded like one she'd overheard once and liked to use now.

We ourselves went out at night now to the pictures and the occasional dance but never, ever did we come across Julia, not even on the long summer evenings spent around the streets and roads of our little town. When few secrets could be kept in that small community, Julia kept hers, remaining forever impassable and aloof from gossiping eyes and ears. She hadn't even a home or family of her own to go to or so it seemed; had no friends that we knew of, yet everyone knew Julia. Her silence was, at times, almost unbearable, so much so that my mother in a frantic effort to determine at least the hour of her return to our house, would resort to putting a tin basin on the landing right in the line of Julia's progress so that the wily one, puffing up the stairs, would hit it a kick perhaps and thus reveal part, at least, of her secret life. Yet Julia, with innate cunning, somehow divined the pres-ence of that basin even in the dark and always managed to skirt it, never as much as giving it a tip to satisfy my mother's frus-trated ear.

Then in the morning, she would be back in the kitchen again like magic, smiling her maddening smile, clad in her volumi-nous garment, all her nocturnal adventures forever sealed be-hind her glistening face. She did her work well into the bargain as far as she was able; not even my mother could find a definite fault although she continued to be certain that, of nights, Julia must be up to no good.

Some years later, a morning did come when Julia wasn't there as usual, hovering around the kitchen in that loose gar-ment; a morning when the doctor called to say bluntly that she, Julia, was now a mother of some ten hours. I ran to her attic, not believing – for how could she possibly! But there, the white-washed walls spattered with blood and the stained bed and garments strewn, confirmed it all. The little wooden door swung sadly open. Furthermore, in the cold, grey, new light, someone had seen her creep along the street with a brown paper bag held close – a bag full of secrets.

But life had to go on. The mattress, sheets and patchwork quilts were burned, the room fumigated by burning a sulphur candle in it, the walls scrubbed and freshly whitened. A new maid was moving in.

My job was to pack up Julia's things and, as I did so, I felt nothing but shame that I now, behind her back as it were, intruded upon her, her who had been so private. Kneeling over a broken, cardboard suitcase, I folded her few remaining garments, carefully placed the half-empty tins of make-up, the lipstick, the scent-bottle with the carnations on it, the dirty combs. Then came the Holy Water and the black book with God hidden in its pages and the little rattly beads – these three I reverently wrapped in a stocking, putting them at the top of the case for maybe she'd need them in this place where she now was, with nuns somewhere deep in the country, along with the baby.

All the way to this place, I thought of Julia and the pride she'd taken in 'keeping herself to herself', and how she'd even managed to birth-struggle alone in a cold, whitewashed attic room so silently, so discreetly that no one had heard as much as a whimper or even an infant's cry.

When at last I drove up the long, tree-lined avenue to a square, grey mansion with pillars on the front steps and big glistening window-panes, I hoped that here, perhaps, Julia would be able to hold fast her treasured hidden-ness which seemed, in the end, to be her only talent, if such indeed it could be termed.

I rang the bell and then I heard the squeaky patter of nuns' shoes on polished wood. A smiling Sister opened the heavy door. I'd come to see Julia please, and so she brought me to a gleaming hallway full of light and flowers. There was a rolling, curving upward stair with polished treads of yellow wood – no room for whitewash here or heated bricks or candle-holders – and coming down them, like a defeated worn-out queen, was Julia. She was smiling still but the loose garment, cross between housecoat and overall was gone (how it had tricked us!); gone too was that imperviousness, that untouchable aloofness. She seemed vulnerable now, her shell taken from her, her secrets all uprooted. She seemed to me, as I stood looking up at her, a faerie thing captured at last, a will o' the wisp pinned down and dissected; for there could be no stealth in this place.

'How is the baby?' I asked foolishly, helpless not to intrude.

'It's a girl,' she said and her face broke into a real smile such as I'd never seen on her before.

'Here's your case. I put the picture of God on top.'

She looked at me as if she was trying to reach the sadness that washed through me, as if she badly wanted to let me know that whether in attic rooms or grey convents, she'd be indomitable still and she took the case from me, asking gravely, 'And the beads? And the Holy Water?'

I nodded and she smiled her old secret smile, 'I like to keep myself to myself.' (Oh! will you be able to, Julia?)

Yet, as I returned home on my own, I knew she would do just that – keep herself to herself in spite of appearances – and here I recalled the old voluminous garment that had hidden the greatest of all her secrets. No matter what would befall her, she'd never be captured, never be pinned down or dissected. Julia would always be free.

I never saw her again although I think of her often and of that little girl too whom I neither saw nor heard named. The attic room of her begetting is now a bedroom with a powder-blue carpet and gentle, shaded lamps, but it may never know again that sure-fire quality of life intensely lived, intensely lost.

CHAPTER SIXTEEN

Christmas

No story of a childhood would be complete without reference to Christmas, that sacred time, that holy hiatus in the year's clutter when time stops briefly as the Divine becomes human and the human Divine and the commonplace hearts of people are flooded with the glorious promise that they should indeed inherit the earth. For this promise was no faraway future thing at Christmas but very present, not the Revelation City of jasper, crystal and gold, of onyx and sapphire and cornelian but the Revelation of the weak mewling of new life born in a stable, our very own life, and with it the assurance that all our life is new life always – every hour, every second gilded afresh by the sentient pulsing power that fills this Creation and heals it even as it wounds it, blesses even as it haunts with its never-dying siren-song of sad sweetness. Christmas: the God/Man Jesus, lowly and majestic, weak and almighty, strong to raise us into the Light so that at this season our heavy human hearts grow light – we laugh, we dance as we are swept up into some kind of heaven-sent spontaneity and lightness of being.

But not for me at the age nine or so were such thoughts of Christmas; nor were they the thoughts of many of us as, without ever understanding why, we felt a new and always unexpected merriment creep into our hearts in the depths of winter so that in our earth-bound calendar, December, the designated month of the nativity, glowed like a fat, bright candle illuminating the darkness of the Cavan winter. Yet December was Incarnation in very truth, all the way from the plucking of the not-yet-festive birds to the holly and the presents; December was the celebration of the great God crept among us without our command, without even our knowledge so that he reigned *incognito* in our own little town in ways that we could both grasp and also recognise as being intrinsic to our own natures.

In those days, the Christmas season didn't start in August with the advertising of venues for office-parties. Christmas started around the first day of December and the letter 'D' at the head of a school's copybook date, seemed the most magical letter in the whole alphabet, for it carried murmurs of another world where life would be transformed and shot through with beauty for a few short days, albeit days snatched out of eternity itself.

I suppose it really began with the goose and the turkey, those two enchanted, almost mystical birds, which appeared suddenly to parade in our yard in the early days of the year's last month, and as we gazed then into the lowering sky, we chanted the ritual chant, 'Christmas is coming; the goose is getting fat, please put a penny in the old man's hat.' And if a few early snowflakes fell, we knew for sure that this meant that the 'old woman' was, somewhere in the heavens, 'plucking her own geese' for Christmas. In this magic, holy month, we believed everything; we knew that the impossible would be briefly possible and above all we sensed with an impregnable surety that no matter what happened 'All would be well, all would be well, and all manner of thing would be well' – although we didn't, of course, know anything about Julian of Norwich whose words these are. As none too pious children, we upheld the doctrine of the Incarnation with all our hearts and gaily entered the kingdom of heaven without even wiping our feet.

As youngsters then, one of the first rites we performed in preparation for the feast, was to traipse around the shop windows after dark to monitor the progress of the 'window-dressing'. This was a rite performed by the shopkeepers themselves, a solemn ceremony, and all participated in it, carrying it out slowly so that it continued over a couple of weeks, one or two little items being added daily or arranged differently. Then after tea, in the early dark, we children, our breaths smoking in the crisp night air, went from window to window around the silent traffic-free streets; condensation on the window-glass made viewing hard but, in a half-circle, tight together, we'd watch in suspense, as adult hands carefully laid down perhaps a toy truck, only to disappear and come back again in a minute with a jack-in-the-box or a doll or a tray of tin soldiers. We could never know what was to come next but each toy, as it was placed down, represented to us a dream that must surely come true. We actually cheered and clapped as each toy was added and called out to each other in voices hoarse with excitement, 'I'm getting that!' and 'I'm getting that!' while the window-dresser smiled at us in delight. Then again, on another night, to our supreme satisfaction, a clockwork figure of Santy would be raised up over the wooden back of the window and carefully placed in the centre front of the growing display. The same Santy appeared year after year and him we would greet with the loudest of cheers as he nodded his head up and down, up and down over a little, creel-like basket that straddled his stomach. The daughter of that shop told us there was actually a real penny in that basket, and how we envied her intimate knowledge of the revered figure.

Other windows were just a little less appealing: in one were rolls of paper chains and boxes of chocolates and a little clockwork figure that appeared only at Christmas and at every Christmas, even though he had no apparent connection with the season at all: this was a little man in a leather apron who not only nodded his head but also stuck out his tongue with every nod! The pubs cheated, we thought, by just putting in a bit of holly round a few dreary-looking bottles and the 'Select Grocers' weren't much better, although these often had strings of little magical lights called 'fairy lights' twined among the hills of dried fruit that lay on the floors of their windows.

At home, there was still more enchantment as our mother got the goose and turkey ready (the goose was for St Stephen's day, the turkey for the 'Big Day'. The birds would have been already plucked and their feathers saved for use in the making of eiderdowns and pillows.) The lid of a floor-polish tin held the methylated spirits and when she ignited this, the blue-purple of the quiet obedient flame was mystical. As she held the birds by the legs and the neck, we watched her matter-of-factly singeing off all the remaining down. The very first exciting part of actually 'cleaning' the fowl had already been accomplished, as well as our examining the contents of the gizzard, where there was never a pearl – just some grey grit.

From this distance in the 21st century, it is almost hard to recall the actual feel of that Christmas excitement then, but it was everywhere – excitement in the house, excitement in the streets, excitement in our own throbbing hearts and tearaway feet. We couldn't sit still but rushed from house to street and back again, afraid of what we might miss. Our letters to Santy would have been written a long time ago on greasy jotter paper, our faces red with anticipation, our tongues curling at our lips as we wrote, and then these letters, with their hopeful lists, would have been whipped up, by a draught, into the blackness of the chimney and whooshed away by a benign wind to the North Pole.

On Christmas Eve (and never before), we decorated our dining-room or 'parlour' as my father preferred to call it. We stuck holly behind the pictures and stretched paper streamers diagonally across the ceiling. Two little paper Chinese lanterns hung at each doorway and, with a wad of cotton-wool dipped in Brasso, we wrote, in giant lettering, an eye-catching 'Merry Xmas' right across the mantlepiece mirror. We never had a Christmas Tree and never felt the need for one – these were used solely for parties in the Parish Hall and perhaps by the more *avante garde*; we ourselves were more than content with what we had.

In the afternoon of the Eve of Christmas, Uncle Jack would arrive all the way from Belfast and because of the season, he would have had a few 'wee ones' on the train-journey so that he always came in looking red-faced and beaming happily while my mother rather quickly encouraged him up the stairs, plaid travelling rug, suitcase and all. We would feel vaguely cheated by his going to bed so immediately because we were very fond of Uncle Jack, but we knew that when he had had his snooze, he would emerge into the house laughing and happy to present us each with a gleaming half-crown.

Amazingly, it never snowed on Christmas Eve, just a soft mizzle to wet the streets and put a web of damp on our coats. Crazily, demonically, we rushed around the small town, taking in all the festive sights, watching the butchers who had moved out now onto the very street itself, counters, scales and all, cold in their heavy overcoats and selling huge slabs of red and cream meat to the farmers who, it was said, ate meat only at Christmas time. By now the festooned shops would be crowded and every-one's humour good. Once I remember that, alone above the crowd, a drunken woman's voice rose and sang out sorrowfully a most unseasonal song: 'The Rose of Mooncoin'; perhaps she thought it was a Fair Day but, to this day, her voice returns to me in a pocket of sadness whenever I hear that song.

As Christmas Eve drew to a close, we children disappeared because we had to listen to Santy on the wireless reading out the names of all those who had written to him before he began his awesome, world-embracing journey this cold, dark night. The glad mysteriousness of it all was almost frightening. Across from our house, a big white candle flickered in every window to guide the Holy Pair to Bethlehem while I myself was always too excited to say even the smallest prayer. Inside, we tidied up our toys, mostly self-made and broken, tidied them as never before just in case Santy might think we had too many already and leave us nothing. Then we went to bed.

Upstairs, the blinds pulled, we lay wakeful in the yellow light listening to the noisy jostle in the street below. As the hours passed, the voices became more raucous and then, at last, the hush that heralded Midnight Mass. I was so appallingly happy then that I was afraid, indeed terrified, that I might die in the night and not be able to gather into my arms the wonders of the morrow. Drowsing and waking again in the still darkness, broken only by a couple of late-night revellers, one playing a trumpet and the other singing, 'O come all ye faithful' in Latin, 'Adeste Fideles', cracking the black and holy silence. At length, finally, finally, down the stairs with us to see what Santy had left – our socks were always stuffed with gewgaws and surrounded by games and books and what did it matter that I'd asked for a doll's pram and he'd brought a little wooden cart instead. His very coming was all and the miracle of the God/Man Jesus was made concrete in small fingers that found him in stockings and tinsel and red-berried holly.

On St Stephen's day, the Wrenboys came to ease the pain of Christmas passing. They came around noon chanting, 'Up with the kettle, down with the pan, give us a penny to bury the Wran.' But later, as darkness fell, the really big Wrenboys appeared in the town having walked all the way perhaps from Kingscourt, seven miles, and these would be merry indeed and not a little intimidating with their crazy outfits and blackened faces and squeeze-boxes and fiddles and tin-whistles all set to entertain us for ever it seemed.

Finally, and it was final, in the 9 o'clock dark of St Stephen's night, the curtains were drawn on Christmas. Tired, we lay in bed then, restless, sad, surrounded still by the toys of yesterday whose magic was now a passing glow. Our mother said her annual and truly hateful words, 'It's all over for another year,' and we sensed her relief so galling to our waning joy. Tomorrow, the shops would reopen, staid and cold and cheerless, stripped already of their so recent glory, and in just another few days, the schools as well, but at least there would be snow to look forward to and, in Cavan, that was almost as reliable as Santy.

CHAPTER SEVENTEEN

Boarding School

At the age of about ten to twelve, my head was full of little else but 'boarding school'. I hungrily read all the schoolgirl books I could find, books where the girls were always collected from trains and taken by car to their boarding-schools deep in the country. In these books, I met benign Headmistresses, very wise but firm Housemistresses, Head Girls, Prefects, House Captains (for the schools were always divided into 'Houses' that competed sportingly with each other in things like lacrosse – especially lacrosse!) These girls did their stint in the classroom but mostly their lives appeared to be spent performing jolly pranks, having midnight-feasts and even solving school-related crimes. They also did a lot of cross-country running and, on the rarest of occasions, they were allowed go to the village shop, although all of them had recourse to ample tuck-boxes! Two or three girls shared a bedroom or, if in a dorm, they had a cubicle each. And there was no mention whatsoever of church-going or religion. They were all really good girls and only the very occasional one had slightly perverted morals just to add interest to the story-line. There were no men in their lives apart from brothers (who went to similar schools) and fathers; the brothers were nearly always 'going up' to Oxford or Cambridge but we were never told what the girls, our heroines, planned to do when they left school with their 'colours' and excellent exam results. I read all these stories avidly, never stopping to think that all this happened on another land-mass, in another culture.

Innocent therefore, I was extremely happy to know that I would follow Mildred and Marguerita, Ernest and John to boarding school (we all attended the same one – except for Lucy, who for some unknown reason was sent to a different school), and the fact that there were boys in this one was interesting, but of minimal importance to me at the age of ten to twelve.

The four older ones had already left this school by the time my own turn came, so I had the experience all to myself, as it were, and, as someone who had always had to share everything with others and be bossed around by others, doing something completely alone and unsupervised by either siblings or parents was a rare treat. It didn't matter that my school pyjamas were Ernest's old ones with the fly sewn up, or that my dressing-gown had once belonged to Mildred and was now a faded green; indeed even to own a dressing-gown was, in itself, enough, for I had never possessed one before. My gym-slip was new and so were my blouses and shoes; my long, black, lisle stockings I tried on with pride noting how neatly they fitted onto the hooks of the 'suspender-belt', another novelty, and I wasn't in the least sad to pass on my old, grey, comfortable knee-socks to Lucy. The blue plaid school rug which would cover my bed had originally belonged to Marguerita who was ten years my senior and it was now quite thin in places. Still I was about to enter a new world, have an adventure, and was undaunted by this or the fact that my outer school coat was home-made and a little lumpy in places, and that my felt beret with the school crest on it had often been visited by moths! I had a school tie too, also a hand-me down and a bit shiny, but my uniform was complete.

Together, my mother and I packed my suitcase and then shut the locks and reinforced the lot with a brown, leather strap. My only disappointment was to do with the 'tuck-box' for, while we did have one in the family, (a long, wooden, oblong affair with a padlock which had obviously been assembled to hold tuck for at least three), my mother decided that this would now be useless. So instead, she gave me a slightly rusty, cylindrical tin box about ten inches deep that would, as it turned out much later, hold exactly half a dozen, newspaper-wrapped eggs and no more.

Thus equipped, I was off on the second leg of my growing-up journey! That journey began on a GNR blue-and-cream bus where I joined about six other returning boarders destined for the same school, not all of whom seemed as pleased as I was for there were some red eyes. The journey took no more than an hour but there was no school car to meet us as in the books; instead we had to haul our suitcases through the town ourselves and up the long, winding avenue to the school itself which, in its appearance, indeed promised much. It was big; it was secluded in the countryside; there were sportsfields; there were dozens of big boys and big girls, all wearing the same uniform; there were the teachers strolling around looking fairly easygoing; and already my thoughts were turning to midnight pranks and secret societies and sporting House Competitions. But alas! there were no 'Houses' – not enough pupils maybe – and I and the other newcomers were not shown to any bedroom or cubicle to unpack our belongings but were bluntly instructed to empty our cases out in a classroom (on the floor and on desks) and then sort out our 'day things' for our 'downstairs' locker and bring the 'night things' up with us to the dorm, where we'd be brought after prayers and supper. (So I needn't have brought my photograph of Lucy after all for I'd have nowhere to hang it!)

I suppose that was the first huge shock: there was to be no privacy at all, no place to be thoroughly alone, except in the loo – and even there you could see 'over and under'. But that first night, nothing daunted, I headed bravely to the dorm at the end of a long, single-line, snaking 'crocodile'. There would have been about twenty-five beds in that huge room with the high ceiling, and windows were so far up in the walls that it was impossible to see out. There were no cubicles or curtains between the beds and I had to stand sideways between mine and the adjacent one in order to make up the bed with the sheets and pillow-cases that had been dumped in a huge pile in the centre of the floor. How quickly I learned to run for those sheets in later days! Otherwise you could be left with some flour-bags sewn together by someone's thrifty mother (maybe by mine!) while your own graced the bed of a girl you mightn't even like very much.

That first night was genuinely exciting. I was one of about eight new boarder-girls and felt an old hand already on account of my brothers' and sisters' previous attendance, and I remember snuggling my face into the little, flat pillow in gleeful anticipation of the morrow and all without the slightest trace of homesickness. I think that was the only time I did the snuggling bit in the five years I spent there.

'Boarding school'! How posh it sounded to those who didn't

go there! How privileged! And since it wasn't a Convent or The Brothers, how grandly Protestant! It *was* a privilege, it's true, for there was no free education then beyond National School, but it was a privilege hard-won by far-sighted parents. Posh? No! Some Protestant schools were indeed posh, but the one we went to was not and there were many others like it. The pupils who went there were mostly solid, middle-class youngsters whose parents had had to make an effort to 'put by' the very modest fees: they came from the same county, from town and farm; there were also a few from more remote and exotic places like Sligo and Tipperary, Donabate and Bray, and most exotic of all, there was among us Maureen Bunnion, the daughter of a Circus Master!

The first form was always quite big but when the Intermediate Certificate exam was over, very few returned to do the 'Leaving', for at that time the 'Inter' was a passport to a good few jobs. In my own case, I started off with about twenty two others in my first year but when it came to Leaving Cert, two boys and myself were all that remained.

Our diet there was poor but sufficient in those post-war years: we had an inch of porridge with bluish milk, along with bread and what we called 'scrape' already on it, for breakfast; no condiments of any kind graced the tables except for a meat-paste jar full of damp salt. Our main midday meal was good: meat and potatoes and a vegetable followed by a bread or milk pudding. 'Tea' consisted solely of mountains of 'bread and scrape' – nothing else – if you wanted jam, you had to supply your own and if you wanted an egg you had to leave it (with your name written on it) in the kitchen an hour before the meal. Fruit was never ever supplied by the school. Before going to bed, we got a half slice of 'bread and scrape' and a cup of sweet tea – for the convenience of the culinary department, it was always assumed that everyone took sugar! And then, clutching our towels and sponge-bags, we'd march, in single-file, up to the dorm, often feeling very hungry; sometimes we smuggled extra slices of bread up in our towels and we'd wash these down with a glass of Andrews Liver Salts, a refreshing drink we thought and on a par, in our opinion, with today's popular soft drinks. Then, under three thin blankets and the rug from home (and maybe a hot-water-bottle that cost us a hen-penny to fill – when we *had* a hen-penny!), we'd chat to each other desultorily in the dark (lights went out at 10 pm). We talked mostly about home and boys, before falling into the deepest sleep I have ever known, a sleep that seemed to last only a minute before being broken by the hateful clanging of the big metal bell in the school yard at 8 am.

Before going down to breakfast, we'd have a *very* quick wash – there was no hot water upstairs and, of course, no baths or showers; after breakfast, there'd be the 'tidy-up' when nails might be checked by a prefect, and holes in our black stockings would be 'mended' with a daub of shoe-polish. Then would come prayers for which the whole school (but only one teacher) would assemble and after that came class.

Now class was terribly important because usually our happiness depended on how we performed in class: we could be brilliant at scoring goals or playing the piano but if we failed to understand the workings of grammar or the principles of an isosceles triangle, we were in for a hard time. My heart often bled for those shy Cavan youngsters who tried to plough through the meaningless declension of Latin pronouns but my heart bled for myself too when it came to maths – I rebelled at the idea of 'an unknown quantity' called 'x'! It was an outrageous notion to suggest that something could be talked about and yet be an 'unknown quantity'. My teachers didn't like my approach and we quarrelled. How I suffered! Ratios, trigonometry with its everlasting 'ships on the horizon', log tables, theorems – it was all an abomination to me and I was punished for my inability to solve these terrible problems. Sometimes, pupils would be called to the board by the maths teacher to do some work with chalk, ostensibly for the benefit of the rest, but if that pupil failed to get things right, he or she could get a few smart cuts of the cane around the shins. Indeed, I remember our being so afraid of maths class that we'd try to escape it by making ourselves faint using a trick that involved a combination of nose-holding and deep-breathing or, if feeling philosophical, I'd just remind myself of Shakespeare's words: 'Come what, come may, time and the hour runs through the roughest day!' – even maths class would end!

Class lasted, with a morning and dinner break, from 9 am

until 4 pm, and between 4 pm and Tea, depending on the weather, we played hockey or just mooched in the classrooms: the boys mooched in the Big Classroom, the girls in three smaller class-rooms. 'Mooching' consisted of reading or just gossiping but sometimes if there was suitable music on the old wireless, we'd practise our dancing for those times when we'd surely be al-lowed to dance again. If we went to hockey, we donned the most hideous, shapeless, garments I have ever come across: baggy, below-the-knee khaki skirts and voluminous tops of the same material; at least the boys played their rugby in normal outfits, striped in the school's colours. Yet, amazingly, I do remember being happy on the hockey-pitch especially on Autumn evenings when I, as half-back, waited while someone practised in goals at the other end: there was that nice, hungry feeling with maybe a boiled egg for my tea and the colours of the leaves and all the lovely Autumn sounds and smells in that country place and the distant voices of children at play.

And how did we clean up after hockey? No showers and no baths. Well, there was a 'foot-bath' – a great, five-feet-square, concrete-lined hole surrounded by a wooden platform which formed a bench on which we all sat together while we scrubbed our muddy feet and legs. The mess was awful and, as we couldn't rinse off, we carried away with us almost as much mud as we'd brought in. There was hot water too in this downstairs area which was a help, but only in two hand-basins.

When Tea came, we were, of course, ravenous and fearful too of not getting enough food or even time to satisfy our hunger. Once we had an eating competition and, to my shame, I won it by consuming twenty slices of bread. I have never tried that trick since and don't recommend it for I honestly thought I would die as a result – the way I felt really frightened me!

After Tea, we immediately sat down to study for three hours (with a ten-minute break) under the supervision of a teacher, and after that it was again supper followed by 'school prayers' and bed. It all sounds at best drab and deprived but I enjoyed it when I wasn't getting into trouble for silly behaviour – not 'bad' behaviour, just the silly and outrageous kind.

While we were cut off from the boys in theory, we made our own adjustments and found ourselves in the position of being able not only to write to them but to speak to them in private and to meet them even more privately still. One locked door separated us from their quarters so when we wanted to speak to a particular boy, we'd rattle the door-knob and, as with a telephone, someone would answer and we'd transmit our message. Often, in this way, you could chat to your boy-friend for ten minutes but I remember that your eye would get watery from the draught at the key-hole. Love-letters were also passed frequently underneath this door which, if they were seized upon by a teacher, would be read aloud to staff to the utter mortification of both lovers. Midnight assignations were also arranged, but these were so terribly risky that they were infrequent, though sometimes we stole out of the dorms in the dark to have a smoke down in the yard – the terror of being caught, however, quite outweighed the pleasure of the smoke.

About twice a year and on the Headmistress's birthday, we were allowed to have a dance in the school but were not allowed invite 'outsiders'. There would be no Prep that night so we girls had loads of time to doll ourselves up. We used mud-packs and powder and eye-brow pencil; we smeared Vaseline on our eyelashes. We'd also have pressed the pleats of our gym-slips the night before by putting them carefully under our mattresses and the boys all donned their Sunday suits so that when the doors opened we were a very shiny, presentable lot indeed. The boys sat on one side of the biggest classroom, and the girls on the other, which wasn't bad for it gave you a chance to see who was coming your way; mind you, no matter who came along you still had to dance – there'd be a teacher there to see to that – and even the tiniest boy still in short trousers had to be danced with by buxom lassies with glad eyes!

On Sundays, we spent three hours in church – two in the morning and one in the evening – we walked a good two miles each way, sustained no doubt by the half-slice of fried bread and the sausage which was Sunday's breakfast treat. Between church and Tea, we wrote letters home, letters that would be read by staff (to check spelling and grammar, we were told!) before being posted, and then we'd set out for a four-mile walk in crocodile, weather permitting, or we'd just read and chat in our classrooms.

One highlight of the school year was the Sunday school soiree which was held in the little Presbyterian Church itself, there apparently being no hall. Here we sat in the pews and were handed sandwiches and buns by smiling church ladies, after which we went back to the school. One year, one of the boys borrowed his girlfriend's felt beret and every time the plate passed he gleefully announced, 'One for me and one for the bag' knowing how glad he'd be of those buns later on. On another occasion, we were all invited to a 'do' in the Church of Ireland hall and being 'the school' we were ushered together to sit at tables at the top of the long room. The tables were heavy with stacks of home-made goodies – sandwiches, fairy cakes, éclairs, tiny trifles in glass dishes, brack spread with butter and so on. Greedily, we eyed the lot and fell to. We ate slowly at first but then picked up such speed that before too long, the Head Girl conveyed a message to us sent urgently by the teacher in charge, 'Tell them to stop eating!' she hissed. She was embarrassed by our hungriness and so, in spite of all the kind ladies urging us to eat up and to have some more, we bravely had to tell them, 'No thank you.' Oh! I'll never forgive the pettiness of that teacher – and just when we were really having one of the very few good times of our lives at that school.

Other good times were when we nearly died of laughter. And we did make a lot of fun for ourselves in what was really a bleak, cold, miserable place, a place without music or art or decent literature, without fires or soft chairs, without places to be alone in; where we felt spied upon, and from whence we never escaped except for the long holidays. (I found a diary many years later that I'd kept when I was fifteen and read a sad little note written on a wretched, cold day in January. It said, 'Going home for the hols this day twelve weeks.') It was a place where we learned, above all things, the power of endurance: to endure the cold, the sarcasm of teachers, the poor food, the pervasive ugliness of everything, the desks which were our armchairs, the knotted wooden floors, the bare walls, 'flu when we were doomed to lie, bookless, under covers in the cold dorm without radio or visitors. But we did make fun and loads of it for we were young and healthy and we all came from good, secure homes which we knew awaited us when school was over.

Then there were the bad times. Times when pupils found they could stand it no longer and ran away. My brother John and a cousin were such: they escaped the school's confines one dark night and walked the twenty miles to Virginia where our cousin lived, making sure to hide behind a hedge whenever a car or a bicycle approached, but when they reached Virginia they were simply returned to the school. My friend Elizabeth ran away too but she was allowed stay at home a while longer before she was eventually bribed into returning. I had a go once, not because I was unhappy, but because I thought it might be an interesting thing to do. So, along with another girl, I strolled casually down the avenue and past the 'Big Tree' (beyond which was 'out of bounds') thinking that the easiest way to go was just to amble off in broad daylight. We got as far as a little path that went from the Head's house to where it joined the main avenue and at this point we were accosted by Miss Pepper who quietly placed an arm in each of ours and led us back to the school saying amicably, 'We don't do this, my dears.'

Of course, as the years went by I rebelled at last; I was threatened eventually with a 'letter to my mother'; my problem was that I was just plain bored. Bored almost to death by the monotonous drabness, the wretched claustrophobia, of the whole regime, it was no wonder that in my last year, with the light from the world outside now at last beginning to beam in, I reformed, became a model pupil and was even made Head Girl – remember, however, that I myself was the only girl in the Leaving Cert Class!

When it was time to leave for good, the last exam over, I went over to the teachers' room to say 'goodbye' one sunny June morning, and am embarrassed even now to think that I cried then. Tears seemed almost hypocritical for surely I had grown to hate the place and yet, on that last morning, I remembered only the good times and knew that another episode in my life was over forever.

I have always had trouble with the finality, the transience of things. I think I have often loved life too much if that can be possible. But I didn't sorrow for long and I remember that Ernest came to drive me away, for good, and with Lucy in the back seat, we sang the latest 'hit' all the way home. It was 'An English Country Garden', a song as full of light and cheer as that school had been dark and dreary. That last morning, an eternity of summer stretched before us and everything was possible.

CHAPTER EIGHTEEN

Cattie

In the days when we were beginning to feel the stirrings of passion for the opposite sex, we began also to take an interest in our 'fortunes', especially as regards our courtships and hearts which seemed forever in need of repair. We fed on romances from women's magazines, sang the songs from the Top Twenty, often alone and with eyes dramatically closed, practically swooning in our new emotions. We saw the occasional really weepy love-film (when we could afford it) and pined for boyfriends that looked like Gregory Peck and John Wayne. There wasn't much else to be done about our desires, and our sex lives were often forlorn and unacknowledged by the society we lived in i.e. except for its unspoken fear of our getting pregnant.

But still there was Cattie, the only woman in the whole town who seemed to be aware of the fact that we might have other aspirations besides going to school, learning Latin and preparing for the Leaving Certificate. Cattie was, among other things, a 'fortune-teller' and without her realising it, I'm sure, she lit up our lives, for to us she was the very queen of 'seers'! She never set herself up as a professional: 'fortune-telling' was just another way of supplementing a miserable income, if 'income' it could be called, for she had nothing at all beyond what others gave her.

We'd grown up with Cattie, had watched her over the years waddle the mile into town, her hair matted under a net, her heavy, shapeless body like a small haycock slung about with the bags where she'd put the things she'd buy, the things she'd be given and the things she'd beg. In summer, her days were usually spent trudging to this house or that farm where she'd been promised a few eggs or a handful of potatoes, her coat always fastened with nothing but a piece of shaggy twine. Often, she also carried a gallon can for paraffin oil, her only source of light apart from candles, and she cooked on turf which she always managed to 'acquire' by means known only to herself.

Ever friendly, ever smiling, you could never really gauge her true feelings since her eyes, a mere twinkle, were sunk deep in the fat folds of her lined face. No one ever laughed at Cattie, no one ever called her names or hurt her. Her tongue, mind you, could be as sharp as a knife if necessary but usually she was too polite for invective or verbal bitterness, so much so that we used to invent stories about her past: was she perhaps some fine Army Officer's daughter born out of wedlock? Or had she been, once upon a time, thrown out of home by pious parents for some little sin – although we could never imagine how this could be, for Cattie's only vice, if it could be so called, was her fondness for Woodbines, those cheap little fags that she sometimes bought in a flimsy, green paper wrapper, five at a time. She could even speak rather grandly at times, put on her posh accent, we said, but she never used bad language and always, to our embarrassment, addressed us young ones as 'Miss'. It never sat easily with us, then, that we in turn should not address her also as 'Miss' but to do so might appear derisory perhaps, because she was not a 'Miss' or a 'Mrs' either – she was just Cattie! To say we loved her would be an exaggeration but we were very fond of her and fervently believed every word she told us about our futures. Yet there wasn't the smallest thing about her to suggest the occult, not even gypsy-earrings or gay scarves but we still sensed that she had 'the gift' and were always wary in case she might throw the 'evil eye' on us.

Her manner of begging was delicate, practised, skilful: she'd approach another person, usually a woman (out of a sense of propriety, we thought) and upon greeting each other – for everyone always greeted Cattie – she'd proceed volubly to admire the lady's pearls or brooch or whatever, telling her at the same time how lovely all of her was. This opening gambit was accomplished so artlessly that the admired one could only smile and offer perhaps the 'few coppers' which was all that Cattie had wanted in the first place, without her having to use the demeaning words.

From our frequent visits, we knew that her cottage on the Kingscourt Road was simply one single room with a rusty galvanised iron roof and was covered, almost incongruously, with rambling roses. Every time we passed in the summer, she'd be there (if she wasn't out on her travels) leaning on a chair at the open door, smoking a Woodbine and she'd encourage us to talk to her across her garden that bordered the road, a garden that had neither hedge nor gate and grew nothing but scutch-grass, nettles and ragweed. In winter, neither the door nor the one window was ever open and Cattie herself was seldom seen and no one seemed to query what she did or where she went – and yet surely someone must have cared?

To tell fortunes, Cattie read the cards but she could also 'do' the cups, and going out to her cottage was to us like visiting a shrine and certainly as exciting, if not more so, as watching Gregory Peck. We'd hardly be in the door than she'd look for the 'screw' of tea-leaves taken from our caddy at home and also the five Woodbines – first instalment of her dues. She could never afford to take chances where these things were concerned and, on our departure, we'd have to 'cross her palm' with silver, a commodity we found it hard enough to come by ourselves.

Once we were inside the cottage, Cattie changed; grew bossy, letting us know who was now in charge of the whole operation and we accepted this meekly for, after all, weren't we being given the privilege of laying eyes on all that she owned in the entire world? In a corner was a narrow iron bed, the bedding a mountain of newspapers. Her fire was in the open hearth where a black iron kettle hung and standing beneath it a saucepan and a tea-pot. There was a table by the window, a chair and a stool, and the floor, as I recall it, was simply hard-packed earth. She sat on the stool to read the cards which she spread out on the end of an upturned butter-box; we were given the chair to sit on when our turn came. 'Now, pay attention, Miss,' she'd say as she laid out the pack, 'The ace of Spades, you'll cross water; Jack of Clubs, mischief; Queen of Clubs, beware of a dark lady; Ace of Hearts, a handsome stranger', and so she'd go on in a rambling stream that was to come to my mind many years later when I first heard rhyming Cockney slang. Each session lasted about fifteen minutes and, as she gabbled on in the fading light (she never lit the lamp in summer), she held the unlit butt of a Woodbine in her toothless mouth, eyes never raised for a second from her work which she took very seriously. Reading the cards was an art-form with her and we never dared to laugh or even look sceptical because we guessed that if we did, we'd be haughtily and at once ejected from that cottage never again to be coaxingly addressed as 'Miss'. Besides, wasn't she revealing our futures, telling us the truth of the gods and, being the wise and kindly soul she was, she never told us anything bad that might worry us. We hung on her words as she spat them out speedily with little jets of spittle, and greedily we watched for the red hearts which, in Cattie's mind, always spelled definite romantic interludes. Better to us was she than the astrology columns in women's magazines that gave us cold, unhelpful information in three or four lines. Cattie brought our future to the present – not, of course the real future which would have been too hard for us to bear – and in the warmth of her presence, chuckling, over-weight and dirty, everything became possible – the whole world was sure to be ours. So, at the end of the sitting, we'd gratefully 'touch her hand' with a little silver threepence and we'd walk back into the town in the dusk, laughing and musing on what she had told us, knowing for certain that life for us could only get better now.

People like Cattie gave us hope in those often miserable and hopeless times when life could present itself, not infrequently, as being full of nothing but coldness and drizzle. She gave us en-tertainment; she gave us laughter; and people like Cattie simply disappeared, unacknowledged. And no! we never bothered checking out the veracity of her tellings; we never kept accounts; it was quite enough for us to know that here was someone who treated seriously the idea that we actually did have hearts, often broken and in need of mending, when other adults simply didn't want to know.

What became of her, I can't really tell but I'm fairly sure she ended up in the dreaded County Home, that hideous barracks of a place just outside Cavan town, a reminder of even more penur-ious times when it had been The Workhouse. And I don't like to dwell on what might have happened to her there: they probably 'dolled' her up, made her 'presentable', gave her floors to sweep while, in her heart, she must have grieved for her cottage, her travels and the visitors who called to get their fortunes told.

The cottage was soon demolished: it was an eye-sore any-way, they said, and a fine two-storeyed house was built on its site but another Cattie never, ever appeared to grace our town; and while, no doubt, fortunes continue to be told, they are not told by her.

CHAPTER NINETEEN

Celebrating the 'Glorious Twelfth' in Cavan

In those far-off days before 'The Troubles' had begun all over again, some little country Orange Lodges sent bands to the 'walks' in the North on 'The Twelfth' to join forces with the big Lodges up there, the Lodges that meant business, the Lodges that were possessed of the blood-curdling Lambeg Drums; for all Lodges everywhere had 'walks'.

The 'walks' in Cavan were held in the Lodges' own fields for those of us who stayed at home, which most of us did and I don't recall ever feeling I'd missed anything by not going north. The very term 'walk' always seemed strange, even then, because you didn't walk at a 'walk': you just went out to this big empty field and bought a few sweets and minerals from the Catholic hucksters who'd, optimistically, I always thought, set up their stalls under the hedges. These much-vaunted 'walks' were invariably awful disappointments for the simple reason that nothing ever happened at them – nothing at all! All the drumming and piping had gone north and we'd mope around the silent, lifeless field in a kind of disbelief that we were wasting a whole afternoon with nothing to keep our spirits up but the prospect of the 'Grand Dance' to be held as usual that night.

To go to a dance on The Twelfth in an Orange Lodge was apparently considered by our elders to be a most beneficial affair altogether and we never disabused them of that notion. It would be an entirely Protestant function and mothers must have seen it as an excellent place for their offspring to meet future husbands and wives. Hence, we hadn't on this occasion to plead for permission to go for it was always tacitly assumed that all Protestants who were still young enough to put a leg out would dance the night long on The Twelfth in an almost imperative ritual! So, of course, it wasn't only the young ones who'd attend these dances: there'd be a few ageing but still hopeful bachelors, a few older women in their thirties in a state of near desperate spinsterhood, along with some fat, comfortable mothers who went to feed the starving revellers.

A fairly factual description of one of these dances must surely disappoint those who may expect to hear of a grand affair simply because it was Protestant, or of a suspect affair simply because it was Orange. The Orange Lodge I remember most vividly was Drumbeg LOL (Loyal Orange Lodge) set on top of a hill deep in the Cavan countryside. So deeply hidden was it that I never once saw it by day, and wouldn't have been able to find my way there without asking directions. About six or seven of us would travel to it together in an old Ford Anglia and I once had to make the journey sitting on the knee of the front passenger, both of us holding our door closed as we bumped and bounced over the narrow, winding sideroads.

On the way, we'd stop at a pub – not always the same pub – (for pubs were strictly forbidden to us!) but one that would be as safely remote and hidden as the Lodge itself, and one that we certainly never saw in the light of day. We could have a drink here any time we liked, no matter how late it might be, because we were *bona fide* travellers i.e. we were x miles away from home and hence ought to have our thirst slaked as was only humane. This *bona fide* business was a great abuse but, in the innocence of the times, great crack too and resulted in our sampling all kinds of dingy, dark and sordid little hostelries.

Once arrived and because there were girls in the party, we'd be ushered quickly through the all-male bar that was filled with smoke, spitting-noises and often with drunken singing, and into the 'Room' which was usually the owner's best sittingroom. Here we'd sit, excited and giggling, in our white shoes and best frocks, their wide skirts stiffened with sugar-syrup; the fellows in their 'Sunday suits'; and among the potted ferns and the antimacassars, we'd boldly sip sherry or even 'gin and orange' – the lads beer or stout – all drinks being served to us on a tin tray by the lady of the house herself. We all smoked our fill of thick, untipped cigarettes whose packets bore no threatening words, and we revelled in the moment knowing gladly that we wouldn't even be expected home before the morning light was in the sky.

It was 'The Twelfth' after all!

After the sojourn in the pub came the dance, so into the car we'd pile again, gin and sherry and all, and away to the Lodge, that little building poised on a hill not like any majestic beacon but more like a bewildered lantern on a ragged bush round which swam a drunken welter of male voices and female squealing. As we parked the car, half in a sheugh for safety, a long, grey funnel of smoky light would pour down to us from the hilltop Lodge, along with the wail of the 'crooner' and the rhythmic stamping of feet in some determined rustic dance. What an assault all of that was on the quiet country night!

Then we'd squelch up the muddy incline to the door, our white shoes no longer white. We'd hand in our entry tickets and be allowed squeeze into the already packed hall which was no bigger than the classroom of the average National School. On the stage, the band would be belting out tunes like, 'She wears Red Feathers', 'Buttons and Bows' and 'Jealous Heart', while the 'crooner' stamped one foot emphatically and in time to the music as he roared into the mike. The floor, when we got there, would be already packed with sweaty, red-faced dancers shuffling through foxtrots, waltzes (old-time and slow), and quicksteps; sometimes a Fling would be called and then the floor would be completely cleared in deference to a pair who could rattle out those steps better than anyone else. Or there might be a 'Paul Jones' or a 'Palais Glide' (we called it a 'polly glide') and now and then, fresh polish would be sprinkled on the floor to make the surface gleam anew – a polish purchased in big canisters from the chemist no less!

At the door, the timid, ageing bachelors would stand watching. Around the hall sat the dazed participants, just looking on now, resting, some too drunk to do anything but sit. The air would be heavy with smoke, alcohol-breath and body-odour, and every so often someone would let off a banger and fill the place with yet a new stench of carbide. The noise would be deafening and it was the most unromantic place in the world and quite unsavoury too. In the midst of all the jostling, pushing and prancing, a maiden or a young man would be hurriedly squeezed out through the door to get sick (courtesy of excess gin, beer or sherry) behind the whins that grew around the door.

Fights often broke out, sometimes over a girl but more often because of an indiscreet reference to a skeleton in someone's family cupboard. But the guards never had to be called to come out on their bicycles and end the fray – neighbours at the dance always managed to sort out the row themselves even though there might be plenty of shouting along with it and the occasional bloody nose. And, overlooking all of this, this wild, raucous, drunken affair, would be a picture of a diminutive Queen of England in a blue dress, hanging crookedly on one of the walls. She could never have known what cavortings went on in her honour!

Half-way through, at around 1 am, 'supper' would be announced and then the aproned mothers (thankfully never ours!) who'd been sweating away in a tiny room off the dance floor would send out boxes of thick delft cups and white enamel buckets filled with sweet, milky tea into which we'd dip our cups as they passed us, seated now in rows on wooden forms. Then would come the mountains of corned-beef sandwiches thick as doorsteps and the hunks of 'curny-bread' to satisfy the appetites of revellers, many of whom had come not just a few miles in an old Ford but who had arrived much earlier by bus after a long day's drumming and piping in the North.

At 3 am on the dot came the last dance of the night and, like all last dances, it could be the occasion of great delight or of total heartbreak. If that tall, good-looking young farmer that you'd danced with already asked you for this particular dance, the world turned into heaven; if not, you pretended you didn't care and just shoved out into the darkness with the tumultuous, heaving throng. The 'courting' came next but because of the unaccustomed stout and the gin and general exhaustion, it was generally short-lived, although future dates for calmer times would be secured. Often the men were terribly shy and the most one of them could manage on one occasion was to ask a girl if she would be 'his pal to the car', the inference being that by doing this, he might be able to put his arm around her on the way.

So really, those Orange dances were not where people aspiring to gentility went, but they were powerful crack and, for weeks afterwards gave us food for talk: this fight and that; Mrs

Dickson threatening to pour tea on the warring Taylors; old Williamson getting off his mark with Big Susan who bleached her hair; and the poor live goat shoved right into the dancehall as a real, but little understood part, of the Orange ritual.

Hard it is now and lonely too, to think that all those ageing bachelors who had pined for a mate on The Twelfth are dead and that perhaps those little buildings themselves have also succumbed to decay. I don't hear them spoken about and I keep meaning to ask but, somehow, it's never an important enough topic anymore. And yet, one day (I promise myself) I will seek out that hilltop Lodge that went by such a colourful name and find that it may well not be there. 'Drumbeg' may live on now as a mere postal address, and maybe there's just a neat bungalow there where the whins once grew.

CHAPTER TWENTY

Home

I can see him still, hobbling with a slight limp around the hay-field, his short, square body bowed over pitch-fork or rake: Joe, the yardman, who had served our family all his life or at least all of mine, for I can't recall a time (before the very end) when he wasn't with us. He seemed ageless to me, this man with the lined, unsmiling face, coarse-featured and moustachioed. When he took off his peaked, cloth cap (which he did only to eat, as though there were some connection between the two!), you could see a yellow, bald patch on his otherwise grey head. Joe was short-tempered and you never took liberties with him; never dared to play even the most harmless trick on this small, gnarled and usually silent man who seemed at his happiest when in communion with our lean, savage, red-eyed bitch called Lassie. He talked to Lassie: long, gentle, rumbling talk when he wouldn't even pass the time of day with Julia who fed him three times a day in the kitchen. And yet, come hay-making time when my father employed other men to help out, these would sometimes manage to draw a few words from him. However, even in the hay-field, he preferred to keep apart, rootling with the wooden rake in his own corner of the meadow; drinking his tea the other side of the haycock. Somehow, just being alone in itself, seemed important to him; it was as though his very nature craved solitude.

At night, he slept in a room in the loft, a room which he kept securely padlocked and it was many years later that I was to enter it and view, voyeuristically, the things he had chosen to hide.

Meanwhile, life for Joe was pretty good even though we thought it must be lonely. He appeared to have neither family nor friends; he didn't go to the pub; didn't associate with the 'corner-boys'; didn't visit other people's houses. His only outing that we knew about, aside from his going to Mass, was his annual visit to the circus; perhaps the fact that the circus always pitched in the field next to our meadow made him feel at home; perhaps, and more importantly, no-one would try to talk to him under the dark canvas while they watched the terrifying stunts.

On dark winter evenings, he retired early to the loft, hauling himself with a pitch-fork up the greasy, moss-covered stone stairs to what we called his 'boudoir', the place we forever wondered about and what it could contain, the place that was strictly barred from our entry. My mother constantly worried that he'd burn us all down with his tilly-lamp or oil-heater for there was no electricity up there, but Joe would have been careful.

He worked six full days a week and did the milking on Sundays, morning and evening, although my father took over the foddering of the cattle on Sunday afternoons; no-one saw anything odd about this for my parents also worked six full days often starting at eight in the morning and going on until nine at night; our neighbours did pretty much the same so it would probably have seemed strange to Joe to operate differently. In any case, he made no great demands on life and I remember how contented he was just harnessing the pony to go to the bog with his bottle of tea and parcel of bread. And I remember too what a little 'general' he was when, with two other men, he commanded the annual ritual of the 'pig-killing'. He always seemed to take a proprietorial interest in our animals. He, who was normally silent and sullen himself, loquaciously scolded these dumb creatures: pony, donkey, cattle and, of course, the faithful red cur, Lassie, who'd let no-one else come near her. He helped the cows deliver their calves, sitting up at night in the kitchen until the bawling started in the byre and then he'd be there to pull out of its mother the wet and curly little thing and set it to rights on its spindly new legs; then when it had suckled, he'd wean it onto the 'beastings', the cow's first after-birth milk. For all this, he received no thanks beyond his weekly wage and this too he took silently. If anything, we grew up in fear of Joe, not knowing that at the same time, he himself was harbouring his own secret fears.

There was that day when I overheard him in the field with Solomon Brown who could always coax a few words out of him.

They were talking about death, or at least Solomon was talking about death, a subject that, at sixteen years, both fascinated and repelled me – the prospect of slipping away into the great unknown terrified me and yet people just went on doing that – slipping into the unknown as if it were the most natural thing in the world. As I listened, it struck me that Joe wasn't too keen on it either. Solomon's news that Billy Hall was dead evoked from Joe not a syllable more than a grunt at first but then, at last, came the question, the telling question; pausing in his work, he leaned on the rake and shoved his cap to the back of his head: 'Where did he die?'

'In the County Home', came Solomon's reply.

Joe said nothing then but I, sitting in the stubble among the skittering, yellow frogs, guessed what he was thinking. He was thinking about the County Home and so, probably, was Solomon. I myself had only heard of this place, this 'Home' and couldn't really imagine what it was like. The one thing I did know was that, universally and among all classes of people, it was a place to be feared: it was to be feared more than the County Hospital where rats ran through the wards (my mother had been a patient there for a week once and had seen for herself); feared more than TB; more even than dying; it was worse than hell itself, for hell was very, very faraway: the 'Home' was only twenty miles up the road in the next town. Not for nothing was it frequently referred to as 'The Workhouse', linked in people's minds as it must have been with its former status in Famine times, as well as with pictures painted by Dickens. Furthermore, we all knew of people who had disappeared to the County Home and had never been seen again: Cattie, the fortune-teller had gone there for one, now Billy Hall and who knew but that Solomon would go there too and maybe Joe as well.

Joe spat viciously over his shoulder now and resumed his raking. Neither man said any more but their feelings conveyed themselves to me and even on that moist and lovely June afternoon, I knew the bleakness, the desolation, the total aloneness of the time of final parting. In my head too that day, a gate slammed.

It was maybe at that time that I began to realise why night after night, Joe climbed up so abstemiously into the loft: why he never smoked or drank; why he didn't even buy sweets. My guess was that Joe was hoarding – hoarding against a dark day. Indeed, I often heard people wondering about the amount of money he must have accumulated by now, seeing as he never spent any, but however much he had, I now understood the reason behind the padlock on the door to his room.

And, of course, the dark day did come. He fell on the greasy steps one October night that was full of drizzle but when we carried him into the house and called the doctor, it was evident that while he was injured, it was nothing life-threatening. Nonetheless, we were instructed to get him to the County Hospital at once and I remember how he limped to the car and sat in the passenger-seat beside me not uttering a word. Now and then, he groaned but he never mentioned his room or the padlock or Lassie or, indeed 'The Home'. There was such a sense of inevitability about it all.

At the hospital, he was quickly taken into custody – that's what it felt like – his pockets were emptied unceremoniously and their contents given to me: some small change and, on a piece of string, the key to his padlock. Then, about a week later, I gathered that he was moved to the County Home itself which was about a mile from the hospital. There was never any other plan of action discussed, there was simply no discussion at all and, to this day, I don't know if he actually died in the Home or if he escaped.

The Home was a giant maw that mostly rendered human beings invisible. I went to visit him there but before I went I had to unlock his room to gather up his belongings and put them in a sack and, while doing this, I found, of course, the piece of paper I'd guessed existed: it was a Bank statement which said simply that Joe owned £500. A lot of money in those days but still not nearly enough. At the Home, they brought me first into a small, damp, official sort of room with a smoky fire burning in the grate, and in this room they took the sack from me – coats and trousers mostly – then they led me to him where he lay in one of about twenty beds in a huge, cold, long ward, ten beds on either side and not a curtain between them. On every pillow was a grey head, eyes wide and staring or, more happily, closed in sleep; mouths invariably toothless and open like little holes in paper faces. At first none of the heads looked like Joe's but then, about six from the end on the right hand side, I recognised him, out of place now and here was I, young and awkward, beside the narrow, iron bed with its very clean sheets and covers. I looked at him, unsure of what to do or say so we said nothing. I put the cake I'd brought him on his locker along with the Baby Power knowing that they'd likely be taken away when I'd gone. I asked him how he was, for I was still too young to endure silence easily and he probably said he was grand. I can't really remember anything else except the leaden quality of sheer misery – a misery, cold, empty and complete that filled the long ward on that lonesome Saturday afternoon. Misery was fanned into life in the space between me and Joe who so barely knew each other: it was a bond.

The green-painted walls were wet with condensation and sent down slimy, silver trickles behind the white beds. The three or four naked light-bulbs suspended at intervals from the high ceiling shed a cold, yellow light. I didn't sit on the side of the bed for that would have been taking liberties and there was no chair nor did anyone offer to get me one. When he dozed, I looked around. I was the only person not stretched out on a narrow bed and I felt ashamed: ashamed of my health and freedom and youth and education, things that would save a person from this place. I felt guilty too: what right had I to be free to walk! No! not just to walk but to run, run out the door, run home to my family and my friends and my books while twenty old men lay helpless and anguished and alone here without even the cold fingers of pity to touch them.

And I did run out. Ran into the sunshine. There was nothing else I could do. Outside, I saw another group of aged men clad in ill-fitting tweed coats once worn by someone else, being marshalled along the gravel-paths by a middle-aged lady in a white coat; they were out of doors for their daily exercise, these old people; well enough to be out but not well enough to look after themselves for, likely as not, they had no family of their own. Round and round they went, heads bent, faces closed, the lady leading them between the neat flower-beds on the way back to their quarters.

Perhaps, like Joe, they all owned £500 and, like Joe, this for them was not enough. Their hard-won savings would maybe find a home with some far-distant relative while they themselves would be safely contained by the pitiless charity of the State.

Outside, I looked back at the grey, stone walls and the dozens of small windows with their diamond-shaped panes; the stout entrance-door, the neat paths, the exit-gates through which many of these old men would never walk again. Suddenly I wanted to cry.

Joe was in no pain when I saw him last; no visible pain. He appeared contented although I knew only too well that he couldn't be, he who had placed such a high value on his solitude. And yet, I consoled myself, maybe in the damp, green silence of that ward, silent save for the hoarse breathing, who knows but that he may have been once again back, in memory, in the hay-field with Solomon Brown on a moist June day with the yellow frogs skittering around him. Who knows?

Postscript:

When Joe left us, my father was already dead some years and my mother was elderly; the children all grown and gone. Joe was never replaced. My mother wasn't able any more for either farming or pharmacy and my brother, Ernest, who inherited the home-place, chose for awhile to keep only cattle which he could easily tend himself while running the shop at the same time.

The days of cheap servants were almost at an end. Yardmen were a thing of the past and maids who lived in attics were replaced by 'dailies': plump, motherly women who came in to do a bit of light housework a couple of days a week. That was in the late 50s. In the 60s, both TV and 'The Beatles' arrived; servants, it seemed, suddenly developed 'aspirations' and people no longer were foolish enough to work six full days a week.

CHAPTER TWENTY-ONE

Gallivanting

'Will you go out round the town and see if you can find Mildred,' my mother would order, 'she's out gallivanting again!' and I'd go out into the misty, damp darkness of the quiet streets wondering what my big sister could be doing to cause my mother so much panic – wondering too what 'gallivanting' consisted of.

But I was never to find out for when I'd eventually track her down, Mildred would be invariably ensconced in someone or other's house having a great crack and a laugh and would never, ever be pleased to see me, 'one of the kids', as she disparagingly called me, come to find her out. So there I'd be, caught in the cleft of my mother's annoyance and my big sister's sixteen-year-old indignation.

To say there was breakdown of trust between them is to put it mildly: neither trusted the other an inch and when Mildred finally got her way and left school early to work in the Bank, my mother was fairly relieved. But even in the Bank, the most decorous, the most taming of places, my wayward sister continued to worry my mother with the tales she told us at home, tales that could only prove that she wasn't exactly an exemplary employee! Who but Mildred would, for example, when passing the Cashier's desk spot the bullseye sweet on his blotter and slip it into her mouth only to find out that the august cashier himself had taken it from his own mouth, oh! just for a moment, to talk to an important customer, and who but Mildred could then laugh a boisterous, loud and unbecoming laugh at her peccadillo when she should have been ashamed to tell it.

Still, she was in the Bank and to be 'in the Bank' was considered to be such a good thing, such an elevated thing that not even my mother dared complain. The unfortunate thing, however, was that Mildred didn't think as highly of the Bank as my mother did, because she didn't give it her undivided attention, a goodly portion thereof surely going to a certain John Sweetman who proved capable of luring my sister away from the mahogany counters and the green shades where she counted her copper into linen bags, luring her away to England above all places, to what dens of iniquity only my mother could imagine.

But Mildred was gone now and no longer could I be charged with the mission of discovering where she went gallivanting. It was all very quiet and I found the evenings peaceable so that I could read my comics undisturbed by calls to go out into the night in search of the wayward one. Yet, I missed her around the place, even missed my mother's little flurries of anxiety.

But the peace was broken one day, smashed outright by a letter. It was a perfectly ordinary letter in a white envelope and I, at once, recognised Mildred's spidery, almost illegible handwriting. It was an ordinary letter that created, for all its size, perfect mayhem in our house. Marguerita was sent for. Marguerita, the eldest, the one with the university degree, the veritable sage in our family, the one with the brains. And when she came, she and my mother went into a huddle on the stairs. I saw them whispering but they didn't tell me what they were whispering about although I knew from the letter arriving that it must be about Mildred. Oh, Mildred! What had you done now? What beyond 'gallivanting' and the sucking of other people's already-sucked sweets and running off to England, could you be up to now? I couldn't tell but awaited the unfolding of the future with excitement, for the future would always unfold and, little by little, disclose its secrets if one were patient.

So I was patient and hence was not taken too much by surprise when one morning the postman threw a bulky packet onto our shop-counter: 'From Mildred,' he grinned cheerfully for everyone knew Mildred and even liked her wilful ways. We gathered around, as my mother flanked by Marguerita, tore open the brown wrapping. We all gasped: there was a very big, framed photograph of Mildred looking truly beautiful in a long white dress, her dimples showing and her thick, fair hair curling to meet the flowers she was carrying; beside her, in a dark suit, stood John Sweetman; and behind them again a clergyman, smiling in blessing over the pair. At some points in life, amnesia sets in and this, for me, was one of them. The shock of seeing my mother so shocked, so utterly bereft of words, was too great for me and I simply forget what happened next. But I did realise that now, for sure, Mildred would 'catch it' because she'd gone and got married in England to that John Sweetman and hadn't even told our mother! So this was what 'gallivanting' came to!

Then followed weeks and months and maybe even much more of a sort of silence that surrounded this sister who was now enveloped in a kind of mystery, a strange aura. The photograph was eventually hung up in the drawing-room so that the neighbours could get used to the idea that Mildred was no longer Mildred, being now, whether we liked it or not, 'Mrs John Sweetman' and had been rendered thus as respectably as possible by a Reverend in church.

But there was no talk of them coming home and indeed I longed for her loud, hearty laugh and her joky ways and I wished with all my being that I could be sent out just once more to see what she was up to now, but alas! the gallivanting had ceased. As for my father, he puffed on his pipe sadly and feared that she thought he was cross with her and I sensed some hidden shame that had somehow overtaken the ebullient Mildred to rein her in at last.

Then one day, and there's always a 'one day', isn't there, when people change their minds and corners are turned and things get forgotten, a 'one day' when it was announced formally and with a sniff that Mildred and John were coming home on a visit. I waited for the days to go in and I hung on the hours, for I badly wanted to see her as 'Mrs John Sweetman'. I wanted to be sure that she'd still laugh at nothing at all, that she'd still do foolish things.

When the door-bell rang, all of us, it seemed, rushed to answer it, headed by my mother and Marguerita. On the step stood a smiling Mildred, her arm through John Sweetman's and there also, peeping through the gap left by their bodies, was a little curly, yellow head, a little thing, born out of wedlock, that was laughing at nothing at all, that looked just like Mildred, and that looked as if it too might, at some future time, like to go gallivanting also.

CHAPTER TWENTY-TWO

Continuing Education

By the time my own turn had come to leave school, my mother had almost begun to despair of me completely as far as my marriage prospects were concerned! She had grown weary of child-rearing having, after all, by now seen four of us already through the Leaving Certificate and on into various careers: Ernest to become a pharmacist, Marguerita to get a BA Mod, TCD as well as one qualification in teaching and another from the London College of Music, John to become a vet. and even the wayward Mildred to have settled into a job in the bank. My mother must have sighed – still two left – me and Lucy (who became a Social Worker) – us two again and, in the end, just me. And I wasn't proving any too promising material for she thought that I also was wild and wayward (which indeed I was for a time) and I hadn't agreed to settle down and marry any of the dozen or so nice, wealthy Protestant farmers in the area as she'd hoped I would. In hindsight, this must have been a terrible disappointment to her, because my getting married or even 'engaged' albeit at the tender age of eighteen, would have put an end to her worries about my future and instead of a daughter who might end up pregnant or involved in a 'mixed marriage', she'd have had a thoroughly respectable daughter living a couple of miles out the road from her and whose husband could now do any worrying that needed to be done.

Anyway when I was just turned eighteen, my mother had already made it quite clear that there was no money left for my further education, (although I didn't really believe her). I pined to go to Trinity College to study Latin and Greek and philosophy and English and wear a gown (as university students did in those days) but no! there was no money left, I was told firmly. So with that idea fixed in place, my mother rootled around in her common-sensical mind and came up with yet another plan: I too would be a pharmacist. For hadn't they that second pharmacy just seven miles away in Shercock and it would only make good sense that Ernest should run the home one and that I should run the other. Perfect sense indeed but for two things: first of all, to enter the Pharmacy College, you had to have two sciences in Leaving Certificate (and I had just one: chemistry and that barely passed); secondly, I hadn't even the faintest desire to study pharmacy. My mother might as well have suggested that I become a jockey! That's how ridiculous and far-removed the prospect of a career in pharmacy seemed to me but, at that time, one didn't argue too much about what one did with one's life. And so my resourceful, energetic mother would overcome not only my own distaste but she'd conquer even my lack of a science subject: I would, she planned, spend a year working in the shop while, at the same time, taking a weekly physics 'grind' in Dublin with a lady called Annie McFadden and at the end of this year, I would sit NUI's Matriculation exam in physics and then be on my way.

I agree now that it was a wonderful plan (beating an arranged marriage) and that my mother had both the astuteness and intelligence to think of it; I agree too that I would probably have been a sight better off financially than I have ever been had I engaged with her plan, but money, career, security, meant nothing to me when compared with Aristotle or the Anglican mystic Dean Inge, whose obscure writings I had just discovered, or the Romantic poets. I remember just how hungry I was then for knowledge, starving for it; I could think of no higher heaven than to sit puzzling out philosophical problems or stumbling through Smith's *Greek Grammar* aided by the minister of my church, in the hope of, one day, being able to read the gospels in Greek.

So to sit every Monday afternoon with Annie McFadden and a physics textbook was not fully in keeping with my dreams. Annie was old, in my eyes, and she probably eked out a living by giving grinds in that rickety old house somewhere in the centre of Dublin and up three flights of stairs; she smoked too, smoked so heavily that her frontal hair was quite yellow and she taught me not a thing even though she did try hard. I almost wept as I listened to her patient, quavery voice going on and on every week about 'sines' and 'cosines', concepts that meant absolutely nothing to me, had no place whatsoever in my thoughts or dreams; and she'd set me homework – I came across some of this many years later – done in the back of a cookery-book above all places – sad little pencil drawings of convex and concave mirrors and numerals set beside them in the form of equations. Couldn't it be foreseen how I would do in my Matric physics in June?

The other weekdays of that pioneering year, I spent 'working in the shop' and this at least had the advantage of reinforcing in my mind and soul that I needed to escape chemist shops for ever and ever, all of them, if I were really to live my life.

I suppose it was an easy enough year's work even though profoundly boring and even though I earned just ten shillings a week and my 'keep'. (To be utterly honest, I did on occasion 'borrow' a little from the till to make ends meet for I had by now begun to smoke cigarettes as was the fashionable thing to do at the time – doctors smoked in their surgeries, clergy smoked on every pastoral visit and so why shouldn't I also smoke – it seemed such a grown-up and smart thing to do.)

I opened that pharmacy every day at 10 am (life was always a little slow in Cavan); swung open the inner glass doors and then got out my bottle of water with the holes punched in the lid: with this I sprinkled water all over the shop's floors, both wood and stone flags, to keep the dust down; next, I got out the sweeping brush and, in turn, raised that dust. No customers would appear too early which gave me time to get started on the dusting and polishing of the thousands of bottles, especially the ones that were exposed to the public view. The pharmacists, my mother or Ernest, would appear a little later although my father, when he was in good health, was usually the first in. After the dusting and the adjusting of the cardboard ads on the glass counters, came the intermittent serving of customers and, as I have said elsewhere, these were few in those relatively impoverished days: a woman for a corn-plaster; a man for a pig-powder and then the earth-shaking prescriptions, would so very slowly trickle in. If my father or Ernest were there, I would be commandeered into sifting glauber salts or packaging those never-ending animal-powders that were concocted from old 'receipts'.

Sometimes my father, with his printing presses in the back of the shop, would be asked to print a few dozen posters announcing 'Monster Auctions' which detailed their smallest contents and these made interesting reading; or perhaps, he'd get an order for tickets for a dance, and if he got none of these and still had a desire to print, he'd start on labels for his pig-powders and my job would be just to stand, patiently handing him tiny sheet after tiny sheet of paper which he'd duly insert into the press, one by one, print, peel off and then stick out his hand to me for the next bit of paper and so on until we had about two hundred of these stacked and put aside to attach to the next batch of powders when they'd be made.

Of course it was all very dull and often when I got the shop to myself and without a customer, I'd make up for it by sitting right on top of the paraffin-heater to read poetry (*Palgrave's Treasury* was a favourite then) or a novel – or sometimes, I'd even manage to squeeze out a few shreds of my tortured, badly-treated soul to make the most sorrowful verses of them.

During that year, my work-schedule was like this: on Thursdays, I went to Dublin to Annie for my grind – this took up the whole day; on Wednesday, I had a half-day; on all other days I worked from 10 am until 8.30 pm and on Saturdays from 10 am until 11 pm. That's how important it was to stay open just in case we might get an extra shilling! And when the shop closed, all the shillings in the till would be counted, the red ten-shilling notes and the green pound notes would be separated and wound in an elastic band and all were then locked into the desk with a note of the day's takings. I don't remember getting any holidays as such, mostly because I didn't really want or need any. For recreation, I walked alone in the country on my half-days – not because I had no one to walk with but because I liked to 'commune with nature', as I called it and could do this best alone. Or at night, I would play table-tennis or badminton in the parish hall; but as far as I can remember, I had no boyfriend that year, having recently quarreled with the one my mother had had her eye on for me.

I also kept the most awful, sentimental, journal full of adolescent emotion and full of odes to various creatures and god-like people; one such ode began, ' O thou fiery creature of Utopia –'!

I was terribly religious, terribly interested in God whom I casti-
gated and implored by turn; and I was discovering all the
strange and sometimes alarming things that were being said
about him by the truly unPresbyterian European philosophers;
but the poetry of Keats in particular was my balm – 'to cease
upon the midnight with no pain' I would sigh out the attic skylight when I had no intention of doing anything of the kind!
There was also time too for a huge written correspondence between me and an old school friend; we wrote twenty-page letters to each other (living only thirty miles apart) describing our
thoughts and feelings and aspirations for she was as poetry-
struck and religion-struck as I was.

It was during that year too that my father's health began to
fail and I worried desperately about him and was petrified at the
thought of his dying. It is hard to remember how I conceived of
death at that time but it was something greatly to be feared and
there was Someone to be met, Someone who'd been presented
as 'love' and who yet would pass stern judgement; 'heaven' had
been shown to me in the Book of Revelation with the result that I
never ever wanted to go to that spooky place; the alternative
was beyond my imaginings. But above all, 'death' was an abyss,
a black hole whence nothing ever again re-emerged. Jesus did,
the Bible said, but that was just Jesus; none of my deceased
neighbours had risen again in three days and walked through
closed doors. My once fervid faith was being questioned.

I sat the physics exam that summer and of course failed by a
couple of marks, but neither my mother nor I were either surprised or disappointed, because both of us, I think, had come to
see that I really wasn't cut out for any kind of shop, let alone a
chemist's shop. In any case, no one said a word in criticism
which was kind of them and then not too long afterwards, as the
result of my minister's advice I think, my mother agreed to let
me go, if not to Trinity, at least to a college in Derry called
'Magee' – the college our minister had attended himself – which
fact alone would have been enough to persuade her, for both she
and all of us thought the world of Revd John Fulton, and it was
he who had already begun to teach me Greek to keep my brain
active during that long, dreary year. In Magee, I blossomed, discovered the immensity of the world and lived in delightful

freefall for a couple of years before finishing my degree course in Trinity. And no one ever mentioned physics or pharmacy to me again.

CHAPTER TWENTY-THREE

Still More Education –in the 50s

Looking back to the two and a half years I spent in Magee College in Derry, I can speak only in raptures. At that time, the student population consisted almost entirely of young men destined for the 'Church' (Presbyterian, of course), a couple of Anglican young men destined for the same and about a dozen young women not destined for anything in particular. I myself, one of the last, never saw myself as being designed for anything other than the relishing of each God-given day. The word 'career' had quite simply and literally never been given room in my vocabulary. It might be thought that I was very short-sighted but my riposte would be to say that I, in fact, lived very wisely, living as one ought to live, totally immersed in the 'Now'.

There was but one Faculty in Magee then: Arts; and one Religion: 'Protestant and Presbyterian'. (When a miniscule Business Studies component was added to Arts, two Roman Catholics arrived, two Persians (Orang and Hooshang) and one Nigerian, David.) As a student body, we were so few in number (about 70 or so) that we all knew each other and were indeed fond of each other as if we were actual siblings. The earnest young Presbyterian men all studied Greek and Hebrew which I myself yearned to study too, but as I was a mere woman, I could only watch enviously as they sweated over the hieroglyphics in their Bibles. Latin was also taught and, of course, the usual other selection of Arts subjects of which we took three or four, my own choice being Latin and English with Philosophy or 'Mental and Moral science' as I think it was then called. The divinity students also took elocution lessons so that the ones from Ballymena, for example, would be taught not to say of their too hot soup that 'it would roast the bake off ye' but would, in the end, be able to deliver fine, stirring sermons in that inimitable Presbyterian tradition with its emphasis on teaching rather than on liturgy or hymn-singing.

We all lived on campus too in fine and beautiful red-brick residences and this brought us even closer together, but we spent our little lives quite apart from the world around us, never knowing contact with the little Maiden City or the people who lived under her skirts. We were out of touch with reality and were more like something out of 'The Arabian Nights' than a very real slice of Derry's history. Magee was just like a liberal boarding-school with good food, soft beds, cheerful fires in bed-room grates and no rules. We were still children finding our feet.

In between lectures (which were usually attended by any-thing from two to fifteen students), many of us smoked 'Gallagher's Blues' when we had the money for them and we discussed 'Life'! At this point we were all totally hung-up on religion which we discussed and researched and quarrelled over – and I suppose practised just a little as we separated our-selves into three camps: the aesthetic/humanist; the EUs (Evangelical Union) and the SCMs (Student Christian Movement). The aesthetes never went near a church or observed the Sabbath; they smoked and drank and were free spirits who preferred to climb mountains on a Sunday while their Presbyterian fellows worshipped in buildings. The EUs, in turn, were very strict: they didn't smoke or drink or dance but instead played parlour-games which brought the sexes tantalisingly near without actu-ally touching; the girls wore no make-up and John Steinbeck was on their mothers' wanted list – to be 'put at the back of the fire' if they could! I used to wonder what these mothers thought of their ordination-bound sons having to read *Sons and Lovers* which was on their English reading list at the time. The SCMs (where I belonged) could smoke their fill, brush with alcohol on the rarest of occasions, wear make-up, dance and talk endlessly through clouds of smoke and over gallons of coffee about 'great minds' and 'great souls' all of which we presumed ourselves to have. The division between the last two 'camps' was so definite that one went to one type of church, the second to another.

In the evenings, the resident students dined together with quaint formality accompanied by unmarried professors, all of us duly begowned and taking it in turn to say the grace; *'Benedic Domine, nos et dona tua quae, de largitate tua, sumus sumpturi per Christum Dominum nostrum.'* And then sometimes after 'tea', a few of the lads, trying to look fierce as they donned new-looking black uniforms and peaked caps, took up guns and told us proudly that they were going out on 'B Special' duty under the guidance of a Presbyterian minister. This meant nothing to us, at the time: indeed we were so totally naïve and apolitical to the point where I myself once – oh! just for fun – broke into the 'Soldiers' Song' at the end of a debating society meeting. My boyfriend was aghast and warned me sternly, and with terrible severity, never, ever to do such a thing again. I didn't.

On Saturdays, we played hockey matches just as we'd done in school and on Sundays we continued to go to church twice. Besides, there was nothing else to do in Derry on a Sunday and I still recall, with a shudder, that awful Sabbath silence broken only by the clip-clop of church-ward high heels and the women's shiny faces and the dreary hats. No shops, no TV or radio, no cinema and, in fact, I myself , rebel though I was, was so well-indoctrinated that it was years later before I watched my first Sunday film – when I was safe on board ship in mid-Atlantic after a brisk Anglican 'Morning Prayer' read by the Captain.

On Sunday afternoons, in between church services, the EUs held religious sing-songs around the residence piano and after that the morning sermon was dissected, thought by thought. Sometimes that sermon would have been delivered by some theological giant but sometimes the students themselves had to preach. On one occasion, a group of SCMs was despatched to conduct service in a church in Donegal. I was delighted to be in that group of students and at once expressed my wish to preach the sermon, but my ardour was quashed – I was a woman and a woman must not preach. I was furious! Any number of silly, un-educated laymen could preach silly sermons both in tents and in churches but a woman must not ever preach not even if she be the land's most acclaimed theologian or the most evangelical of Christians. To preach, a woman must first be 'ordained' and there was, at that time no sign whatever of that happening. (Presbyterian women would make good wives for ministers and I might have been one such myself had not my beau, sensing the radical in me, warned that if we were wed, I must run the Women's Missionary Society meetings the way he wanted and not according to my own ideas.) As it turned out, however, the Presbyterian Church was, in the end, the first church to ordain women (late 50s I believe) and if they had done that while I was at Magee, I would today be a minister in that church. As it was, I received, in Derry, only a thorough grounding in the training of future ministers which was interesting but not terribly useful as I'd never get to actually do any of it.

CHAPTER TWENTY FOUR

Emigrating

Such were my first couple of university years, at the end of which we proceeded to Trinity College to sit 'Littlego' exams. Trinity came as a mighty shock! I remember how totally overwhelmed I was by it all: its immensity; its anonymity; its grandeur; its air of decadence – and I was just a wee girl from Cavan who for two years had romped in an almost unknown college called Magee in that wretched outback which was then Northern Ireland. Suddenly I felt ashamed and piteous and yet, stubbornly refusing to show any senses of inadequacy, I hid beneath the drabbest outfit I could muster, clothed myself in navy, grey and black: to look as dowdy as possible was my way of saying, 'I don't belong here and I don't want to belong.'

I have no happy memories of Trinity and sadly, in fact, I learned very little there: the lectures I went to were dull and badly attended and the people I met all seemed to speak a kind of BBC English. I remember the Elizabethan Room, however, in particular; this room was off Front Square and reserved for ladies only; it was full of chintzy sofas and armchairs and the ladies who apparently studied here, also engaged in a little desultory conversation on occasion. Of course, these ladies were all middle-class Protestants, like myself indeed, given the state of our education and religious systems and they were a pretty class-conscious lot. One of them talked of how dreadfully shabby it was that Trinity was beginning to be infiltrated by the 'bog-trotters' (the very word she used that afternoon) such as had habitually gone to UCD!

While I was a student in Trinity, my life in general seemed to close down. I stopped going to church (forever, I thought) and all the shiny heritage bestowed on me by Cavan Presbyterianism ebbed away – no light left anymore, no sense of gladness and it seemed as if all the radiance of a blessed childhood had been blacked out. Nothing left now it seemed but a barren atheistic lunar-like landscape. God was gone; had folded his tent and moved away leaving me to long for his presence even as I cursed him for his absence. As a child, I had been seen to be the relatively holy one and wasn't it ironic now that while all my siblings remained faithful church-goers, I had jumped ship!

Relieved but somehow feeling thoroughly let-down by life in general, I graduated with a lowly pass Arts degree, took a deep breath and then headed for Cook's in Grafton Street for my ticket to Canada on the Cunard's *Ivernia*. I would move on!

A month later then, suddenly subdued and all grown-up, I arrived in Cobh where I was to stay overnight in order to board the ship. It was July 1958, I was twenty-two years old and Cavan was far away. Cobh was abuzz with travellers and their relatives that warm summer night; these were no package-holiday people for no one yet, it seemed, knew much about 'luxury cruises'; these were real, live emigrants, a breed seldom found in that genuine sense anymore.

I had never been on a ship before, apart from a short crossing between Larne and Stranraer on the *Princess Victoria* (later to go down). But now I was emigrating to Canada, first stop Quebec City and then disembarkation at Montreal. I had two suitcases, both brightly labelled, one label reading 'Not Wanted on the Voyage'.

It seemed a long time since that day when I had finished with Trinity College for good. I had no notion of what lay immediately ahead. In the more distant future and unqualified as I was, I'd a job waiting for me in a primary school in Ontario (the School Board had already paid my sea-fare) but on the morrow, I only knew that I'd board a tender that would take me and the other Irish out to the ship which was due to lie off Cobh. just as *The Titanic* had done not so long ago. I felt fearless and confident, brimming with excitement at having begun what must surely be a huge adventure for any healthy, unattached twenty-two year old! I wasn't in the least homesick either, nor did I spare a thought for the family left behind, not even for my now widowed mother (such is the thoughtlessness of youth): fond 'goodbyes' had been said and life must go on. Briefly, I tried to identify with the emigrants of the 'coffin-ships' but they were too far removed from *this* Cobh.

There were probably about thirty of us emigrants now waiting – mostly Irish – and all morning we stood huddled in groups
beside shabby suitcases at the water's edge, waiting patiently to
be told when we could board the tender, the timing of which depended in turn on the arrival of the *Ivernia*. None of those whom
I met were sophisticated travellers: none had been to North
America before; and Europe, of course, at that time and, to people of our ilk, was even more remote being the haven of the artis-
tic, the cultured, and the wealthy TB sufferer. And we were all,
as I recall it, inappropriately dressed: the men in good serge
suits and ties; the women in suits and high-heels; there were no
children at all; accents were thick and guttural: we were all
mostly from the 'country' apparently.

When we were finally allowed on the tender, we watched
carefully, anxiously, to make sure that our entire luggage followed and then, inside, we huddled, headscarved against the
mist in a little open-sided cabin where we were given hot tea
and biscuits. We all talked non-stop, high on adrenalin, squint-
ing at the horizon; and then, at last, out of the rain she rose like
magic: 'The Ship'! There in front of us, the gigantic black and
white *Ivernia*, dotted with port-holes under crimson, smoking
funnels, gay with a multitude of little flags and bunting, waiting
to receive us and how truly honoured we felt as the band on the
deck played, 'When Irish Eyes are Smiling'! In a dream-state, we
moved up the gangway into the ship's open side and I remember how breathless and stunned I felt at the transformation that
then took place: one minute we were in a bobbing, leaky tender;
the next, we were in a 'warm place' that was filled with light and
mirrors, carpets and paintings, music and smart black-and-gold
uniforms – not to mention the pervasive British accent which
continued to awe us in spite of ourselves.

The tender was gone now, never to be seen again by us; we
were off at last to North America, no longer mere Irish citizens
but partly British for awhile since we travelled on that country's
soil, so to speak, and when we'd arrive in Canada, we'd be given
even newer labels. But that was a whole week away.

As steerage passengers, we shared cabins, four to a cabin at
most and we only got to *hear* about things like 'the Captain's

Table' but a full list of fellow-travellers given to us all revealed that we shared this ship with veritable 'Rockefellers'!

As voyages go, that very first one was promising to be un-eventful but, as though it were specially laid on for us first-timers, just two days out, a major storm blew up which threatened, at the time to end my sea-faring days forever, so frightening was it. It was nothing much at first. Just the ship swaying and creaking a little more than it had been doing all along; then, ominously, the stewards in the dining-saloon putting up the fiddles around the table-edges to keep the dishes and cutlery from crashing to the deck; this was followed by a definite emptying of places at mealtimes while the ship creaked and swayed all the harder.

One well-travelled gentleman told me I should thank God that the rivets in the ship's fabric were creaking so loudly for this meant that they were doing their job well; he told me I must worry only if that creaking were to stop; others reassured me that the whole ocean out there, now grey and tumultuous, was absolutely choc-a-block with shipping – we had company after all; we were not alone! But I do believe we all thought of *The Titanic*. Next, the decks were forbidden to us and the ship began to heave mightily from prow to stern as well as from side to side; the Captain no longer appeared at night in a social capacity at his table and we drew some comfort from knowing that he was on the Bridge instead. In an almost deserted lounge, a woman sat on a chair in the very centre of the floor pretending to read when suddenly the vessel bucked and reared going over to one side and, with an almighty crash, took tons of sea, slap into her hull. It sounded like the mighty thud of many guns being fired all at the same time. The woman screamed and dropped her book, 'Oh, my God! We've hit an iceberg!' She was eventually calmed by a steward while I, sick with fear, definitely heard the strains of, 'Nearer my God to Thee'. Through the giant port-holes in the lounges, it was impossible to differentiate between the sea and the sky so great was the tumult and the interplay of elements.

All that night, I sat alone in the corner of a great, deserted lounge, alone except for one other woman who shrank in another corner; we were too frightened even to talk. I sipped a fizzy drink through a straw – I think this must have kept me from being sick – but I would not go down to my cabin, my mind being too full of *The Titanic*. The band-members were all sick and in the ghastly screaming and rocking, the cymbals rolled out from behind the curtained dais in the lounge and went clattering across the deck. That storm lasted seventy-two hours and I vowed I would never set foot on a ship again as long as I lived. Before we finally disembarked, we were each given a copy of the ship's log and learned that during the height of the storm, the waves had been fifty feet high. And yet, when it was all over and the sun shone again and the air grew warmer, the officers serenely exchanged their black-and-gold uniforms for white ones, while we passengers rapidly resumed our gaiety as if nothing at all had happened.

It is difficult to describe how it was to see land for the first time in a week, to slow down and sway rather lazily up the St Laurence. Land! I had thought never to see it again and, foolish as it may sound, I understood a little of how Columbus must have felt. It should be remembered, of course, that I hadn't yet seen television and the New World was just a place on a map or a picture in a book. Of course I knew there was a country called Canada and of course I knew that people lived and worked there and yet it was a genuine shock to me to see long, colourful cars (the pink ones especially) silently cruising the distant roads that ran alongside the great River. Cars! Roads! Tiny figures of people in fields. All seen by me now as if they had been newly-made in Eden's garden; it was just like, quite literally, arriving on another planet.

Soon the immigration-officers came on board and, of course, the pilot who directed us to a place off Quebec City, green-coppered and towering, where some passengers disembarked to be taken to land by yet another tender. Then on up-river to Montreal.

Now it was at this point, when the immigration-officers boarded the ship off Quebec City, that my political status changed. I was now precisely 'an immigrant'. No longer significant was my proud citizenship of a distant Irish republic. I was given a new label, a somehow slightly demeaning label that told me in bold letters that I was now a thing called a 'Landed Immigrant' and in it, I felt, was implied the notion that I should moreover be grateful for it. But those officers couldn't have been kinder: they made sure that I knew exactly where I was going; they booked ahead for train-tickets and wished me well; yet I felt, somehow, disrobed, I recall, as I continued my tremulous way to Montreal to find, if I could, the Canadian Pacific Railway Station, to be borne away across territory big enough to terrify me even on a map, to a new and totally unknown place now to be called 'home'.

Montreal was very hot and very humid that July day; the temperature was a mind-boggling 87 degrees Fahrenheit and I bewailed the fact that no one had warned me. Now here I was fresh from my cool green fields clad in a blue jersey-wool suit from Switzer's with stockings, suede shoes and gloves and a lit-tle mushroom-coloured handbag containing strange notes and coins whose value I could only guess at. At this point, I almost wept for the *Ivernia*.

Once seated on the strange and very long train, I was con-scious of being stared at: perhaps it was my rosy complexion outstanding among all the deeply-tanned faces with their very white teeth; perhaps it was my accent, obviously well worth lis-tening to, I thought resignedly; in any case, I felt very isolated, embarrassed and profoundly lonely. (How well I can empathise with our immigrants to Ireland these days and see how badly they are treated by comparison.) Timidly, I moved through the sea of eyes, all smiling and friendly, to the dining-car and, in yet another new seat, tried to appear composed as I gave the waiter my order: I'd have roast beef, please, and a pot of tea – even I knew that this sounded a strange order but it was the best I could extract from the lengthy garble of French and English on the menu. Everyone round me stared again, stared and smiled. I didn't think it was very funny and I blushed like mad while try-ing to appear calm as if I wore jersey-wool suits, gloves and stockings on Canadian Pacific trains every single roasting-hot summer. The beef, I remember, came along first along with a glass of iced water – and the bill! I nibbled at the beef in what I thought was a nonchalant, suave manner but I was too anxious about that little bit of paper in front of me to enjoy eating; be-sides , sweat was trickling out of every pore of my body! Finally, with all eyes upon me, I boldly but furtively, turned the chit over. My worst fears were realised! I simply hadn't enough money – not nearly enough! I seemed to have been equating dollars with pounds and my entire book of crisp Travellers' Cheques, purchased so carefully in Bailieborough, lay snug in my suitcase in the Guard's van! Now, the carriage was almost awash with compassion and as the waiter zoomed down the aisle to another table, I timidly tapped his arm and whispered, 'Please forget about the tea.' He smiled at me, all kindness: of course he understood---no problem at all, and the whole carriage smiled too. Then, unbelievably, he took up the bill, adjusted it and put it face down beside my plate saying cheerfully in those lazy Canadian tones, 'Oh, you'll have your tea for sure, honey; it's coming right up!' Again I looked at the wretched chit and again I knew I simply couldn't pay. Moreover the beef was now eaten and tears seeped into my eyes. I was only a 'landed immigrant' after all and what else should I be feeling but lonely and lost and, above all, utterly helpless. What would become of me in this huge foreign train that roared across strange countryside bringing me to a strange destination? Oh, why hadn't I stayed at home with the old familiar GNR buses and a country that I knew inside out? Then a man, who was drinking soup across from me at my table, did an unexpected thing! Without a smile, without a glance or a word, he pushed a $20.00 bill in front of me and behind it, his business card. Both items lay flat and discreet among the dishes and fully hidden from the horribly interested eyes in the carriage. So I paid for my beef with that money (didn't wait for the tea!) and left the dining-car with the business card in my handbag, tearful and full of gratitude for the generosity and tact of a total stranger who had not only lent me money but had saved me my dignity by giving me the means to repay him which I did, of course, the next day.

And so it is that these days, happily back in Ireland, whenever I come upon refugees, I am reminded of how it was to be a little like them once, just a little, for I have never been hurt as they have and, in my own much smaller loneliness, I was received into the Canadian community with a warmth and generosity that I can only interpret as love. Thank you, Canada, you kindest of countries.

It's a sobering thought to realise now that we Irish, who have for so long prided ourselves on our hospitality, are able to give so very little to those who come from other countries who seek shelter in our land; we who, in our turn, have received so much. To emigrate is difficult enough but to be an emigrant and a refugee at the same time must be too awful to comprehend and yet, we Irish have been there too, which makes it all the more difficult to understand how our collective, racial memory comes to be so short.

CHAPTER TWENTY-FIVE

Lost and Found

I settled into my new life quickly but, during the following eight years in Canada, I found that not only had I left Ireland behind but I had slipped free from all the religious strictures and restraints that had carefully insulated me from apostasy. During my eight years in this new country, I developed my career and trained as a psychotherapist but I didn't darken a church door although I was haunted by a continuous sense of Godlessness, of forsakenness. I went to an occasional Quaker meeting, tried the Unitarian Church and sauntered through the streets of Montreal after the saffron-robed monks as they called on Krishna. I read all that I could lay my hands on about other faiths, Buddhism in particular, for I was no longer a Cavan Presbyterian. What I was or who I was or where I was going, I hardly knew but I felt smaller and more lost than I'd ever felt in childhood.

'Better to have loved and lost than never to have loved at all' – but no! that wasn't true where God was concerned, for this sense of 'lostness' tormented me. Day by day, it tormented me. For hadn't there been a time when, as a small child, I had been so near the gates of heaven that I really did come 'trailing clouds of glory'; a time when my close-to-infancy days were not broken up into 'morning', 'noon' and 'night' but came as a continuous, unbroken outpouring like the benediction of a holy universe. Hadn't there been a time when God stumbled along beside me as I myself had stumbled on three-year-old legs; hadn't he been in the trivial grittiness and small hardships of my sunny childhood; hadn't he crawled and played, laughed and sung, filled me with light and omniscience as I'd played with shells on beaches?

But it was the 'emigrating, the 'growing up' that changed everything. It was the discovery of 'doctrines' that had caused me to challenge and even to censure this God of Abraham and of Isaac and of Jacob. It was the 'doctrines' and the 'theories' that caused me to upbraid him, deny him, denounce him; in truth, he was nowhere near; not 'dead and risen' after all as the Presbyterians had taught me; this God in Christ seemed a fake. It appeared, confusedly now, that there were really two Gods: there was the God of my innocence who was not a sham (he would be 'real' forever and ever) but this 'innocent God' was not the same as the One that the preachers had seemed to preach when, from their pulpits, they thundered about 'might and majesty', 'dominion and power', about judgement and hell's fire. The God who still lurked in my being bore no relation to the shibboleth of the churches – not as far as I could see. So year by year, I looked for him in nature, in philosophy and theology, hunted for him in every faith and creed. I heard whispers of him everywhere in Christianity (especially in the writings of Evelyn Underhill). I sensed him in Buddhism, in Hinduism, in Islam and Judaism, but nowhere found the One who had revealed himself to me when I was that child on Laytown beach.

Then, one day back in Ireland for good, I came upon a book written by a Church of England bishop and read some amazing words that let me in on the secret about the *one God* who turned out to be Allah and Krishna and Yahweh and Christ and whose home was the entire cosmos: the *one God* only who ran in humanity's veins, our Life-blood, our Breath and our Pulse, our Creator and our Creativeness; the *one God* who played with children on wet sands and, by example in Jesus Christ, empowered us even to die for each other. This *one God* was, after all, the same God as the God of the churches in spite of the thunderous preaching, and I thought that perhaps the preachers might lay more emphasis on God's union with his creation, on his incarnation; and how he is always on his knees with us in our human detritus and our bloody pain; and then too how he can make us cry out in an ecstasy of sheer joy at life itself.

And all this was happening in me as I went about leading an apparently humdrum existence and which I talk about now only to explain the leap I seemed to make from an 'agnostic secularist wildness' to 'quiet faith'; from being a laid-back and careless 'drifter' once upon a time in Cavan to my seeking 'holy orders' in the Church of Ireland. Nor was this latter ever a case of my rejecting Presbyterianism, which I loved dearly and which had nurtured and nourished the spirit in me as I grew up. But it was, in the end, simply a mundane matter of 'geography' that I turned to the Church of Ireland, there being no Presbyterian Church within easy distance of where we live. I could have turned to any of the other Reformed Christian churches, their theology being all the same, but there was something about the Church of Ireland: my mother and her wonderful *Book of Common Prayer* for one thing, and the sheer beauty of the Anglican liturgy, along with that church's willingness to think outside itself. Moreover, my husband is a member of the Church of Ireland. Thus it was in this church, a church I had come to love as I attended its services with my husband, that I eventually sought ordination (and what a long, long time that took me); so that under its wings I now serve where I can and am myself nourished.

At last I had reached the place in my life when I must tell the world about the love of Christ as I experienced it, a love that is not simply 'nice' or 'pious' or 'respectable'; a love which is not just in church pews and church organisations but a Divine cosmic love that gets dirtied with all of humanity's dirt, that touches the untouchable and keeps time with the beats of our most irregular and wayward hearts; it's a love that anoints little children. It was time for me to share, with my own few loaves and few fish, that divine love that has always fed me even at times when the very wilderness-manna seemed to be withheld.

In that providential childhood of mine, there had indeed been room for roots to sink down and to send up, eventually, beautiful blooms and worthy fruits with which to nourish and sustain future generations. And I thank God for all in that little town, Bailieborough, who nourished me: Cattie and Julia and Joe, my parents and brothers and sisters, along with the Presbyterian Church, my minister and friends, especially the children of the 40s.

And the present children? Well, they need a special 'PS'.

CHAPTER TWENTY-SIX

P.S. For today's Children in Bailieborough

None of you knows this town of yours, although you think you do and although you even play in the same space, attend the same school, walk the same streets as I did. Our town, now yours, is completely gone. Your town is full of cars and the Main Street is no longer a playground; the footpaths where we played with marbles are now fashionably laid-out in ugly brickwork so that marbles can no longer roll on them or hopscotch-beds be drawn on them; you have a swimming-pool on the Galboly Road where we once watched Bamboozelem play with his monkeys and where farm-boys full of lemonade after a day's work got sick in the swinging-boats. Your streets still have the same names but the people who live in them don't know me anymore; my people are gone, most of them, and when I walk your bricked footpaths, I feel invisible, walking through a ghostly, deserted past.

And, children of today, can you imagine how wonderful it was to *own* your town? To feel welcome in every house? To know fantastic characters called Kruger and Kank and Jambun; or Auntie Ma, Paddy Da, John Joe and Aggie? Dame Maid and Gabby Annie; the Borry, Pat the Puss, Paddy the Scut, and Joe the Spoon? And how comforting and comfortable it was then to walk in and out of other people's houses without having to ring a bell or telephone ahead? No, of course you can know none of these things; none of you were born in time; you missed out!

In the Main Street where you now live, the tall, and not so tall, houses lean together in their multicolours, leaning against each other as they did in my day, seeming to lean in also over the very street itself so that they give the impression of forever being in a huddle together to watch over all the goings-on. It was an airy little town then, so full of space and time that Tuesdays could only be identified by the arrival of the 'comics', and Sundays by the Sabbath silence and the wearing of suits.

Onto the Main Street converged the lesser streets: Church Street, the Old Green which wasn't a Green at all and yet was probably the most vivacious of all the streets with its tiny, cramped houses out of which tumbled a humanity not clothed by respectability but by its own vesture of earthiness; Barrack Street, the Post-Office Square and Market Square; Thomas Street, Australia Street, Adelaide Row, the Institute Road and a couple of others whose names were nondescript. But it was on Main Street that the people of all the other streets, and from the country too, assembled at some time or other every day of the week so that by watching from a doorway or window any afternoon, you could tell who had what for their dinner or tea; you'd know who was sick, who was dying, who'd got a summons to the Barracks. You could tell too which farmers came to town and which farmers' wives bought new coats the day they got their egg-money.

The shops, of course, have changed: many owners dead or migrated to the now more fashionable countryside. I don't remember all of them but I do remember those who for one reason or another told a story and did so without realising it. There was the Bicycle Shop where you got a puncture fixed by a merry, curly-haired little man who laughed a lot and was invariably full of cheerfulness; in its place is now an anonymous modern house. Further up the street was a shop from which, on occasion, would emerge a tousled little altar-boy with a surplice under his arm, late for Mass, and his father already setting out the grain-sacks on the sunny footpath. There was the shoe-shop, its shelves white with cardboard boxes and the shop-boy who lay in wait for us as we ran to school to lure us in to the dark, leather-smelling squeakiness while his master and mistress were safely eating potatoes and cabbage in the kitchen behind the shop.

Next door was a pub with nothing in its closely-guarded, green-meshed window but a great picture of a seal with a bottle of Guinness balanced on its nose. A lean, grey woman called Maggie lived here beside her posh neighbours of The Corner House Drapery, with its fine marble lettering. This was the Dockery establishment where they sold men's clothes on one side of the shop and women's on the other. And I remember how Mr Dockery took bad one night and Mrs Dockery had to run all the way over to Dr Carroll's in her nightdress. What a wonderful picture that was to me as a child: a white-flapping, frightened figure running alone, barefoot no doubt, through the dark, silent night to get help for her husband.

Crossing the road at the Green, where once I was almost run over by McDonald's bread van on its way from the bakery on the Back Road, you came to Mullaney's Select Grocers that seemed forever destitute of customers. I recall this shop particularly because it had a bacon-slicer, not an electric one, but a fine bacon-slicer nonetheless, a fine shiny, metallic business securely screwed into the counter and, as a small child, I was once sent by John to ask for the loan of this bacon-slicer. I don't remember the outcome.

After that came Daddo's, where we threw our hats up the stairs through the open door just for the fun of retrieving them without being caught by Mrs Daddo, her hair coiled neatly round her ears in two, grey catherine-wheels. Daddo was a severe man with a veneer of charm, and stern, serge, pin-striped suits; we kept well out of his way.

Other shops, other houses: one where an aged aunt teased a myopic boy, toeing away from his searching fingers the sweet he had dropped; and a wealthy owner of a grocer's shop who, invited for Christmas dinner, was asked to lend a tin of peas for the nonce, and on New Year's Day billed her hosts for the same peas. There was the man who couldn't enjoy his home-made soup unless he could see the 'sheep's eyes' floating on top, and the barber who cut our hair even though we were girls, with an ash-dropping cigarette always hanging from his lip. The poshest butcher's shop was a cold, cold place to which we went on Saturday mornings to collect the Sunday joint, and the butcher was cold too, his face blue and his nose red and always a drop hanging therefrom.

Then, if you were cold or needed to collect a watch from the jeweller's, you went, of course, into Jemmy Armstrong's. Jemmy was a little dark man, maybe a little dirty man but that made no odds for he kept a shop that was like an Aladdin's Cave, full to the brim with timepieces of every description and, since he never opened a window, none of the heat from his paraffin heater escaped nor did a breath of cold air ever enter. So it was a dark, warm, fetid place full of vapoury breaths and full of people collecting or delivering their clocks and watches or just full of country people who had come to the town and needed a bit of heat and a chat. The light inside the shop was never out and no one was ever behind the counter except Jemmy himself. A slight, neat little figure dressed in black, with black apron and black 'gutties' on his feet, and an eye-glass screwed up at one eye, he jigged, in a kind of dance, continuously up and down behind the counter examining clockwork and forever chanting in an audible but hushed monotone: 'Watches and clocks! Watches and clocks!' while on the other side of the counter, his customers lazed in a great fog of cigarette smoke and much breathing and much conversation. What is in its place today? A shop that sells ice-cream and papers.

Then there was the hotel which, as a child I called 'the hottle' for it rhymed, I thought, with our chant: 'Hittle hottle/porter bottle/ *out* jumps the cork!' It was an important building by the standards of the day, its most distinctive feature being the decorative wine-red and white glass awning at the front door which announced that not only was it a 'Commercial Hotel' but a 'Temperance Hotel' to boot. We didn't think of the owner as a hotelier: he was just the man of the house who spent most of his time running his grocery shop which was nextdoor while his wife, for her part, ran the Temperance Hotel itself which meant that she simply fed 'commercial travellers' and gave them beds to sleep in. In the shop, hung a very large picture of a clock's face and underneath it the caption: 'No tick here!' I always liked to stand and read that notice and admire the pun which I thought was so very clever and discreet. And so, where now sits a suave receptionist taking bookings for weddings and discos and weekend breaks, and where now black-garbed waiters run swiftly from bar to lounge, was once the very place where a sedate mild-mannered couple sold 'select groceries' without 'tick' while they also, at the same time, produced wholesome Irish stew for 'paying guests'.

Then further up the street, tucked up on the top floor of a house in the Market Square was Misso Byrne's who sewed for half the town – who made my eldest sister's wedding dress. I loved to visit her premises which was just one solitary room but a room so arranged as to be both spacious and cosy: cunningly fitted out with bed and sewing-machine, kettle and open fire, dresser and table. Misso Byrne herself was tiny – like a little elf – and was forever in a good mood. Near her premises was the shoemaker Joe and his wife Leesha and their disabled daughter, Joan; these too seemed untroubled by the world and always treated us with the greatest of kindness and indeed courtesy: here again was a shop where country people liked to rest as they waited for their shoes to be completed and there was always plenty of chat for, in those days, the 'ones from the country' needed to rest in the town and to be entertained a little after a journey of up to four miles on foot or bicycle.

Everywhere there was room for talk. Our 'TV' was what went on in the streets and in other people's houses (the real thing hadn't yet arrived) and it ran in an unending series: we didn't have to wait for another week, for example, for the next episode since the story was continuous and we never thought that the story would end for, at that time, nothing ever really ended, and moreover, since those days were happy days, you could say they were a foretaste of heaven.

There was the little ice-cream shop on Barrack Street with its notice that read, 'I scream/you scream/we all scream/for Carolan's ice-cream' and nearby it the house where the grandfather could speak fluent Irish. Before we got our own phone, we often got calls from boyfriends on the Guards' phone in the Barracks and, in later years, when the Squad Car arrived, all shiny and new, it sometimes took my brother Ernest and his friends out to fodder the cattle, the Guard/driver in full uniform.

There was the forge in Thomas Street where the sparks flew, and the AOH Hall where I saw my very first film – *Snow White* – which was so real to me that I spent the rest of my life looking for a repeat and was always disappointed to find only a cartoon. There was also the lady with the very white hair so respectable but reputed to love whisky; this lady was used as an example of the power of prayer at one of our Saturday Meetings for it was said that after a period of prayer with a 'reformer', she was persuaded to empty her full bottle down the sink. I always wondered if she just went out then and bought another.

As we grew older, our interest in our neighbours only increased and when we got our first car (always parked right outside our shop), we passed many hours just sitting in it, watching the people go about their business. It was of huge interest to us to see that Miss Jones, who was a 'Spirella Agent', sometimes forgot to draw the curtains when her customers fitted on their new corsets in the room over her shop. It was also fascinating to watch Pinnim Welsh selling his fish in the Main Street and hear him shout, 'Herrin's alive; their mouths open! Pipes in their mouths and them smokin'.' We noted the long, sideways step of big Mag who complained of the cold even in summer and assured us that we'd never 'get our winter drawers off us the year, daughter!'

One greatly-loved man was 'the dreamer' who never seemed to do anything much but stand at the edge of the footpath outside his house, study the world on the street and weave philosophies about it; he was so idle and so wise, always giving, rarely receiving. We told him our joys and our sorrows and he always had a few poetic lines to suit every one of them. In the height of what he called 'mad July' with its shimmering heat, he'd head down to Lear River for a swim at his own private place, and then later on, as we, (with that sweet, youthful sadness) felt the passage of time, particularly on hazy summer evenings, he'd think of Shelley perhaps and, with a fag dangling from the corner of his lips, would console us softly with the poet's words: 'We look before and after and pine for what is not.' One time when I 'discovered' Zen Buddhism, I found what I thought was a haiku written especially for him; it was, 'On the temple bell/resting, asleep/a butterfly.' He smiled at it and liked it.

We also loved to brag about our town! It was the highest town in Ireland; it was the coldest, and the people were the meanest and cutest and most 'through-other' even the 'dirtiest'. We'd have none of your fancy, new-fangled litter-bins dreamt up by bodies called 'Tidy Towns'! And the idea of a time when we'd be part of one big European Continent appalled us. For what then would become of our characters? Paddy the Scut would be working in Geneva, and Cattie, the fortune-teller, would be stationed in Paris while strangers would take siestas on our broad Main Street, and sharp, no-nonsense Germans would click their heels outside Jemmy Armstrong's. No! We were just fine as we were, thanks very much! The Roman Catholics had their AOH Hall and their Parish Hall; Protestants had their Presbyterian Hall and their Church of Ireland Hall; there was a building at the top of the street called the 'Masonic hall' and I never knew what that was about although Protestants did dance in it now and again and Catholics were not allowed into it. In our various Halls, we played badminton and put on concerts which consisted of stage-plays with local castes; these were very popular and we rolled around with laughter to see Joe Pratt swaggering on the stage in a policeman's uniform saying the most unlikely things, enjoying him more than we enjoyed the actual play! There was also a cinema and we went there the odd time when we had the money: it was small, dark and full of fleas and always smelled of disinfectant; there was no balcony so nothing separated the serious film-goer from the wild, unruly band of children (and adults too) who cheered and upbraided the figures on the screen as they saw fit. But it was always warm in there and in those days, when heat was scarce in every house, the cinema was a good place to be: one local lady was reputed to go every single night and had 'squatter's rights' on a seat where no one else dared to sit. Then there was the circus once a year and sometimes a Freak Show. I remember well going to one of these shows: there was a tent, and outside the door a notice that read, 'Come and see Miss Ima Waite, the world's fattest lady: admission 4d'. When we went inside, there she was, incredibly obese, literally mountainous, overflowing the seat on which she'd been placed on a platform, apparently unmoved by the row of incredulous faces that stared up at her; she just sat there, patiently knitting as we got our 4d's worth. What a cruel world it was, at times! The only redeeming factor was our ignorance for we knew nothing about eating disorders or glands or hormones – or even human bondage.

But that's all over now. Even memories fade but right now, you young ones are weaving your own memories; creating right now the lives that will sustain you and your own children in the future; you too will spin out your tales from the threads of whin and briar and drumlin and be nourished by the sheer goodness that abounds in that place for goodness will always abound there; and you too are dreaming *your* dreams, not our dreams, old and faded, but your own: shiny, new hopeful and just as beautiful. And you will find too, if you wait for him, that God always runs alongside you and if he seems to hide awhile as you grow older and perhaps a bit cynical, you will discover, if you are patient and if you are content to wait some more, that he has never left at all; and remember above everything that maybe he is most readily encountered in your own ragwort-filled fields and among your own little green hills.

CHAPTER TWENTY SEVEN

The Peak

About a mile and a half outside that little town of my growing-up, was 'our' mountain – hardly a 'mountain' at all but since it was high up and untracked, covered with heather and rocks, we liked to term it 'The Mountain'. *Loch an Lae* was its formal name and up here, we could feel the wind on our faces and look back down at the little rutted roads we had climbed in our effort to reach the top, look back down towards the clutter of distant houses and smoking chimneys surrounded by the stitched-together green patchwork, while above us, the very heavens seemed always within reach of our innocent fingers. On Bilberry Sunday, a day named like a saint's day and, certainly to us, it was indeed a sacred day, we trekked up from town and country-side on that August Sabbath to pick the bilberries which flour-ished on their little scrubby bushes.

Loch an Lae. Our 'mountain'. And this day, as though from its peak, I look back through eyes, now septuagenarian, at the windy little paths, crooked and uneven that I have climbed up (it was to be always up) from pure childhood and heartsweet youth to maturity and I know that, in a very definite sense, my soul, my mind, my entire being has been touched, been tinted, by that lively, sticky sap that flowed though all the lives I en-countered on the way: the people, the animals, the plants; for-tune-tellers, curly-brown calves; shoulder-high cow-parsley: their life flowed into my life and filled me, uniting us, me and them, forever.

And the Sabbath mornings sitting in the polished brown of the pews in our little Presbyterian church shaped me too. It wasn't enough for me, even as a child, to gaze at the one stained-glass window with the shepherd and his lamb bright with sun-shine; not enough to hear the music of the holy words pour out their beauty from the King James Bible; for there was Loch an

Lae to be reached like that biblical Mt Sinai whence Moses viewed the Promised Land which was now my own Sinai, my own zenith, if ever I could attain it.

The dreamy days of *Beano* and *Dandy*, the farmhouse visits, seaside holidays, solitary musings on long summer days, the chanting of tables in sleepy, sunny classrooms where stray wasps buzzed, all worked together to create the fibres that would strengthen me in the climb up out of that little market town, the place on which, almost seventy years later, I can look down, look back and be astonished at the glory of it all. For, without a doubt, I have been accompanied all along by that very Shepherd whose colourful glassy representation beamed in on our Sabbath singing, flooding with rainbows the black print of our black hymn books. Nor has it always been a broad way: I fell heavily often, struggled up again, stumbled on, cut and bruised and downcast; while sometimes the very clouds lay on my shoulders, swamping me, overwhelming me in their grey wetness; yet always I knew that I was going upwards – somehow upwards towards a benign mountain-top light.

Slowly I learned that the almost crazy joy of my childhood and the wild spontaneity of youth could be called by the name of 'God', for after all what else could be the source of such extravagant, such overflowing rapture but God who comes in many guises. It was God, the all-pervasive animating mystery, who had beamed such light on that little town of my growing-up so that it became for me the 'heavenly city' of the Book of Revelation. And it was this same God who, in the end, compelled me and enabled me, not just to stand on top of Loch an Lae among the bilberry bushes, not just to admire the biblical Mt Sinai but to spill out the glory and exaltation that engulfed my being, to spill it out in torrents to the world so that others might perchance catch some drop of it.

And so now, in my seventy second year, I know for sure that God is the alpha and the omega, the beginning and the end; he drew me with gaiety through childhood; was steadfastly with me in those often chaotic and down-at-heel middle years when I so often despaired, and is with me still so that 'old age' is a grace-filled age and just as magical as those years I described at the beginning of my life-journey. There is indeed a grace here now; a steady sense of belonging to the world, of being an essential, inherent part of it. I am one with the trees and the birds and the sky – no longer merely an observer; one with my fellow-humans; and, as I walk by the sea which I do almost every day, I am satisfied, deeply satisfied, by the knowledge that its ebb and flow are my own ebb and flow and that the ebb is quite as wondrous as the flow; that death is quite as wondrous as birth. No longer looking objectively on life, I am unified in life and have one imperative only which is to reflect the glory I have found; to sit down and pause awhile with my fellow pilgrims on life's journey, to eat their broken bread and share my own and give the hurting ones a hand along the Way.

I don't go back to Cavan often now; my mother has died and the old home is 'gone' although still physically there and, amazingly, it's still a pharmacy run by my family 'the Jamesons' while a plaque on the wall testifies to the birth there of Francis Sheehy Skeffington. The streets are full of cars now; there are zebra crossings and traffic lights and oh! what sadness I feel as I walk those streets where we made mud-pies and played hop-scotch and where I was called 'good gersha', because now, not one person recognises me. I feel like a ghost, completely invisible, as the people I meet take me for a tourist – not even a 'whoorist' as one old character of long ago put it!